P9-DND-924

SPECTACULAR
CAKES

Mich Turner

Spectacular Cakes

Photography by
Janine Hosegood

Universe

I dedicate this book to the boys in my life –
my husband Phil, my son Marlow and in
memory of William. Together you are my
eternal inspiration.

First published in the United States of America
in 2005 by Universe Publishing
A division of Rizzoli International Publications, Inc.
300 Park Avenue South
New York, NY 10010
ww.rizzoliusa.com

First published in the United Kingdom in 2005
by Jacqui Small LLP,
an imprint of Aurum Press Ltd,
25 Bedford Avenue, London WC1B 3AT

Text copyright © Mich Turner
Photography, design and layout copyright
© Jacqui Small 2005

The right of Mich Turner to be identified as
the Author of this Work has been asserted
by her in accordance with the Copyright
Designs and Patent Act 1988.

All rights reserved. No part of this publication
may be reproduced, stored in a retrieval system
or transmitted in any form or by any means,
electronic, mechanical, photocopying, recording,
or otherwise, without prior consent of the publisher.

ISBN-10: 0-7893-1361-8
ISBN-13: 978-0-7893-1361-4

Library of Congress Control Number
2005903670

Second Printing

2006 2007 2008 / 10 9 8 7 6 5 4 3 2

Printed and bound in China

Publisher Jacqui Small
Editorial Manager Kate John
Editor Anne McDowall
Designers Maggie Town and Beverly Price
Production Peter Colley

contents

introduction

Welcome to my first book on spectacular cakes. The designs included here can be adapted to create perfect cakes for a variety of special occasions, including weddings, anniversaries, birthdays, christenings and bar mitzvahs. Whether you are a novice or a more experienced cake decorator, I hope you will be encouraged to re-create these designs using the detailed instructions and photographs as well as inspired to design your own spectacular cakes.

There are several things to bear in mind when choosing or designing a special-occasion cake. Firstly, what is the event? Who is the cake for and what would be their preference? Will the cake be traditional or contemporary in design? Should it be something formal or more fun and funky? Does the occasion call for a tiered, perfectly iced cake or would a sculptural chocolate creation studded with chocolate-dipped fruit be a better option? You should also take into consideration the venue: tents can be particular hazards for multitiered cakes – opt instead for a stacked cake or perhaps a chocolate helter-skelter; time of year – a light summer pavlova or a rich chocolate truffle torte?; number of guests and the mood of the occasion – create a cake with drama for a large social gathering or use individual cakes presented on a tiered stand for a more intimate setting. Consider, too, the colors, flowers and particular themes that have been chosen for the event.

In addition to the above, you'll need to decide on the flavor of the cake (see cake recipes, pages 12–19), its size and shape, and how to stack or support a tiered cake (see pages 34–7). But the most important thing is to enjoy your cake decorating! It can be immensely comforting to bake cakes and cookies to share, and even more satisfying to decorate a special cake – and it often means so much more to the recipient to know how much time, love and attention you have devoted to it. I challenge you to have a go!

Mich Turner

cake techniques

cake preparation

A truly spectacular cake starts with a well-baked cake. In this book you will find cakes baked in many shapes and sizes – round, square, oval, heart, hexagonal and petal shaped. It is well worth taking the time to line your pans properly and accurately to produce a cake with a good, even shape. The recipes included in this book are all tried and tested at Little Venice Cake Company for our range of special wedding and celebration cakes. A special wedding cake is usually served after a substantial banquet. Cakes with intense flavors will stand up to a champagne toast, will reignite the taste buds, and your guests will not have to eat a huge slice for their palates to be satisfied.

Cakes should generally be covered for two days and stacked the day before you wish to decorate them. Fix ribbon around the boards after cakes are decorated.

tiering cakes

Because the cake recipes that follow have a more dense texture than some other cakes, they are able to provide support when presented in tiers. Always position the more dense cakes at the base of a finished tiered cake, reserving the lighter cakes for higher up. A rich fruit cake will support the weight of the other tiers, adding stability.

In order of density, beginning with the lightest, the cakes are as follows:

Coffee and walnut cake (page 14)
Luscious lemon cake (page 15)
Chocolate truffle torte (page 13)
Moist carrot cake (pages 16–17)
Traditional rich fruit cake (pages 18–19)

While it is feasible to have a 5-tier cake constructed from 5 different flavors, I have found providing a choice of 2 flavors to be practical and sufficient.

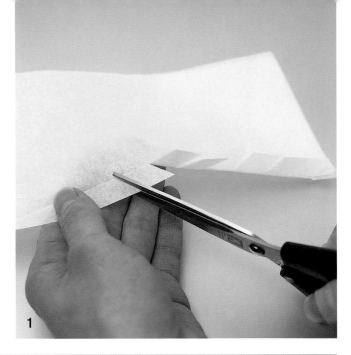

lining the pans

1 Take a piece of waxed or parchment paper at least twice the size of the bottom of the pan and fold it in half. Place the pan over the folded paper and draw around the bottom in pencil. Cut out the 2 pieces just inside the pencil marks. Fold a sheet of waxed or parchment paper long enough to line the circumference, or all sides, of the pan in half lengthwise, making sure it reaches at least ¾ inch above the top of the pan. From the folded crease, turn up ¾ inch and press hard to form a sharp crease. Cut diagonal snips along the folded edge of the paper up to the crease.

2 Brush the inside bottom and sides of the pan with sunflower or peanut oil. Place a paper disk in the bottom of the pan. Gently ease the strip of paper inside the pan as shown, pushing the diagonal snips into the edges and corners. Brush around the snips with oil and place the final disk of paper on top. (Line a square or other shaped pan in a similar way, making sure that the corners fit neatly.)

you will need

cake pan

parchment paper

pencil

scissors

pastry brush

sunflower or peanut oil

Tip When baking the rich fruit cake, fold a piece of brown paper in half and tie it around the outside of the pan with string. This prevents the sides of the cake becoming overcooked.

cake recipes

These cake recipes all have an intense flavor with a rather more dense texture than a standard cake. The chocolate, lemon and coffee and walnut cakes work well particularly, whether they are covered in marzipan and icing or lathered with smooth glossy chocolate and served for dessert. Ingredients quantities given are for a round or square cake.

chocolate truffle torte

This chocolate truffle cake is made with melted chocolate and its texture is similar to a chocolate brownie. It's delicious split and filled with chocolate ganache buttercream (see page 23), which gives it extra flavor. You can then cover it with marzipan and icing and hand decorate it or, for a decadent dessert, cover it with chocolate ganache and serve with fresh berries. There is comparatively little flour in this recipe, which relies on the chocolate and eggs for support. The cake is baked as two layers; this ensures that it cooks evenly while retaining an overall height of 3½–4 inches. As an alternative to a large cake, make individual cakes of 2-inch diameter by stamping them out of a single layer. Quantities given below are for round or square cakes.

ingredients	6-inch	8-inch	10-inch	12-inch
semisweet chocolate (70% cocoa solids), broken into pieces	7 oz.	14 oz.	1 lb. 5 oz.	1 lb. 12 oz.
unsalted butter, softened	9 oz.	1 lb. 2 oz.	1 lb. 10 oz.	2 lb. 4 oz.
light brown sugar	12 oz. (1⅞ cups)	1 lb. 8 oz. (3½ cups)	2 lb. 5 oz. (5¼ cups)	3 lb. 7 oz. (7¾ cups)
large eggs, beaten	5	10	15	20
vanilla extract	1½ tsp.	1 tbsp.	1½ tbsp.	2 tbsp.
all-purpose flour, sifted	5 oz. (1¼ cups)	10 oz. (2½ cups)	15½ oz. (3⅞ cups)	1 lb. 4 oz. (5 cups)
bake convection 275°F conventional 325°F	45 min.	1 hr.	1 hr. 20 min.	1 hr. 40 min.

1 Preheat the oven. Melt chocolate carefully in a microwave or in a bowl over simmering water, then allow to cool. Have all the ingredients at room temperature. Grease and line 2 cake pans. Beat together butter and sugar until light and fluffy. Add beaten egg, a little at a time, beating between each addition.

2 Pour the cooled melted chocolate slowly into the creamed mixture, beating all the time. Stir in the vanilla extract, then fold in the sifted flour.

3 Spoon mixture evenly into pans and bake for the time stated. The baked cakes should be well risen with a crust but should still wobble when shaken gently. Remove cakes from oven and allow to cool before turning out onto a wire rack. The crust will sink back onto the cake.

To store This cake will keep for up to 10 days once covered and decorated or wrapped in waxed paper and kept in an airtight container. If you refrigerate it, allow time for the cake to come up to room temperature before eating it. It is also suitable for freezing – allow to thaw overnight.

To serve When you are ready to decorate the cake, you can simply sandwich the 2 halves together with chocolate ganache buttercream. For greater luxury, slice each cake horizontally in half and sandwich with a further layer of buttercream. (This is only advisable if you are able to serve the cake with a plate and fork.) For individual cakes of 2-inch diameter, split one cake horizontally and sandwich halves together with chocolate ganache buttercream.

coffee and walnut cake

This coffee and walnut cake is wonderfully sophisticated. Part of the reason for its delicious appeal is the use of the best-quality ingredients – California walnuts and real espresso coffee. Don't be tempted to substitute instant coffee granules here: the cake will taste much better – and be more indulgent – if you include a cup of real espresso. The coffee and walnut flavors are enhanced when the cake is layered with coffee buttercream and covered in glossy dark chocolate ganache for a true mocha experience. This is also a simple cake to make, thanks to its all-in-one method.

ingredients	6-inch	8-inch	10-inch	12-inch
unsalted butter, softened	6 oz.	12 oz.	1 lb. 2 oz.	1 lb. 7 oz.
superfine sugar	6 oz. (¾ cup)	12 oz. (1½ cups)	1 lb. 2 oz. (2¼ cups)	1 lb. 7 oz. (3 cups)
large eggs, beaten	3	6	9	12
self-rising flour, sifted	6 oz. (1½ cups)	12 oz. (3 cups)	1 lb. 2 oz. (4½ cups)	1 lb. 7 oz. (5¾ cups)
baking powder, sifted	1½ tsp.	3 tsp.	5 tsp.	6 tsp.
ground coffee	2 tbsp.	4 tbsp.	6 tbsp.	12 tbsp.
boiling water	½ cup (3 tbsp. espresso)	¾ cup (4–5 tbsp. espresso)	1½ cups (5–6 tbsp. espresso)	2 cups (6–8 tbsp. espresso)
California walnuts, chopped	3 oz. (⅔ cup)	6 oz. (1⅓ cups)	8 oz. (1¾ cups)	11 oz. (2½ cups)
vanilla extract	1 tsp.	2 tsp.	3 tsp.	4 tsp.
bake convection 325°F conventional 350°F	30 min	45 min.	1 hr.	1 hr. 15 min.

1 Preheat the oven. Have all the ingredients at room temperature. Prepare 2 cake pans – grease and line with waxed or parchment paper. Beat the softened butter for 1 minute in a large bowl with an electric mixer until light and fluffy. In a French press, pour the boiling water over the ground coffee and allow to infuse for 2 minutes. Plunge and pour the concentrated espresso into a small cup.

2 Add the sugar, eggs, flour, baking powder, espresso and vanilla extract to the butter in the bowl and mix together for 5 minutes until light and fluffy. Fold in the chopped walnuts. The mixture should drop easily from a spoon.

3 Divide the mixture between the prepared pans and bake for the time stated until risen and light golden in color. A skewer inserted into the center of the baked cake should come out clean.

To store This cake is best served and eaten fresh but will keep up to 4 days once covered and decorated or wrapped in waxed paper and kept in an airtight container. If frozen, allow to thaw overnight.

To serve When you are ready to decorate this cake, simply sandwich the halves together with espresso buttercream.

luscious lemon cake

This lemon cake recipe is light and refreshing, which makes it a lovely addition to any summer event and perfect for serving after a rich banquet as it refreshes the palate. It is also versatile: you can slice the cake horizontally in half and sandwich the halves together with lemon curd buttercream, then cover it either with marzipan and icing or with smooth chocolate ganache for a delectable dessert. As with the other cake recipes, it's important not to skimp on quality of ingredients. Although there are a lot of fresh lemons to zest and squeeze, the finished cake is well worth the effort!

ingredients	6-inch	8-inch	10-inch	12-inch
self-rising flour	5 oz. (1¼ cups)	10 oz. (2½ cups)	1 lb. 2 oz. (4½ cups)	1 lb. 12 oz. (7 cups)
all-purpose flour	5 oz. (1¼ cups)	10 oz. (2½ cups)	1 lb. 2 oz. (4½ cups)	1 lb. 12 oz. (7 cups)
unsalted butter, softened	7 oz.	14 oz.	1 lb. 10 oz.	2 lb. 8 oz.
superfine sugar	7 oz. (⅞ cup)	14 oz. (1¾ cups)	1 lb. 10 oz. (3¼ cups)	2 lb. 8 oz. (5 cups)
large eggs, beaten	4	8	15	22
zest of lemons	2	5	9	14
fresh lemon juice	2 tbsp.	¼ cup	½ cup	¾ cup
vanilla extract	2 tsp.	1 tbsp.	1½ tbsp.	2 tbsp.
for the syrup glaze:				
lemon juice	about ½ cup	about 1 cup	about 1½ cups	about 2 cups
superfine sugar	3 oz. (⅓ cup)	5 oz. (⅔ cup.)	8 oz. (1 cup)	11 oz. (1⅓ cups)
bake convection 275°F conventional 325°F	I hr. 25 min.	1 hr. 40 min.	1 hr. 50 min.	2 hr. 10 min.

1 Preheat the oven. Have all the ingredients at room temperature. Grease and line the cake pan. Sift flours together. Beat together butter and sugar until light and fluffy. Beat in eggs a little at a time, beating well between each addition. Add a few tablespoons of flour to prevent mixture from curdling. Carefully fold remaining flour into the creamed mixture. Stir in lemon zest, juice and vanilla extract. Spoon the mixture into the prepared pan and bake for the time stated until risen and light golden in color. A skewer inserted into the center of the baked cake should come out clean.

2 While the cake is baking, make the syrup glaze. Strain the lemon juice into a small pan, add sugar, stirring all the time, and heat gently until sugar dissolves. Remove from heat. Once the cake is baked, remove from the oven and pierce with a skewer several times. Spoon over lemon syrup then leave cake to cool before removing it from the pan.

To store This cake is best served and eaten fresh but will keep up to 5 days once covered and decorated or wrapped in waxed paper and stored in an airtight container. If freezing, allow to thaw overnight.

moist carrot cake

This carrot cake – baked with walnuts, rum-soaked golden raisins and coconut – makes a lovely, lighter alternative to a rich fruit cake. Once the cake is baked, it is spiked with a fresh citrus syrup, which helps keep it moist and fruity. So, too, does the use of sunflower oil, and because the recipe uses no dairy products, it is suitable for guests with a dairy intolerance. I used this recipe for the wedding cake I designed and made for Pierce Brosnan and Keely Shaye Smith and – at their request – I added chopped candied ginger. Although no filling is necessary for this moist cake, it does taste particularly good if split and layered with fresh orange buttercream (see page 23).

ingredients	6-inch	8-inch	10-inch	12-inch
dark rum	2 tbsp.	¼ cup	⅓ cup	½ cup
golden raisins	4 oz. (⅔ cup)	7 oz. (1¼ cups)	11 oz. (1¾ cups)	14 oz. (2⅓ cups)
all-purpose flour	6 oz. (1½ cups)	12 oz. (3 cups)	1 lb. 2½ oz. (4½ cups)	1 lb. 10 oz. (6½ cups)
ground cinnamon	2 tsp.	4 tsp.	6 tsp.	8 tsp.
ground nutmeg	1 tsp.	2 tsp.	3 tsp.	4 tsp.
baking soda	1 tsp.	2 tsp.	3 tsp.	4 tsp.
sunflower oil	⅔ cup	1¼ cups	2 cups	2½ cups
superfine sugar	3 oz. (⅓ cup)	6 oz. (¾ cup)	8 oz. (1 cup)	11 oz. (1⅓ cups)
light brown sugar	3 oz. (7 tbsp.)	6 oz. (⅞ cup)	8 oz. (1¼ cups)	11 oz. (1⅔ cups)
large eggs, beaten	2	4	6	8
zest of lemons	1	2	3	4
zest of oranges	1	2	3	4
carrots, peeled and grated	6 oz.	12 oz.	1 lb. 3 oz.	1 lb. 8 oz.
shredded unsweetened coconut	2 oz. (¾ cup)	3½ oz. (1¼ cups)	5½ oz. (2 cups)	7 oz. (2½ cups)
chopped walnuts	2 oz. (½ cup)	4 oz. (1 cup)	6 oz. (1½ cups)	7 oz. (1¾ cups)
vanilla extract	1 tsp.	2 tsp.	3 tsp.	4 tsp.
chopped candied ginger (optional)	2 tsp.	1 tbsp.	1½ tbsp.	2 tbsp.
for the citrus syrup:				
light brown sugar	3 oz. (7 tbsp.)	4 oz. (⅝ cup)	6 oz. (⅞ cup)	8 oz. (1¼ cups)
juice of lemons	1	1½	2	3
juice of oranges	1	1½	2	3
bake convection 275°F				
conventional 300°F	1 hr. 30 min.	2 hr.	2 hr. 30 min.	3 hr.

Tip When lining the pan, ensure the baking paper is at least 2cm (½in) above the height of the pan. Once the cake is skewered and the citrus syrup is poured over, it will appear flooded. This is perfectly normal and all this delicious juice will be absorbed into the cake.

1 Pour the rum over the raisins and leave to infuse for 1 hour. Preheat the oven. Have all the ingredients at room temperature. Prepare the cake pan – grease and line with waxed or parchment paper. Sift the flour together with the ground cinnamon, ground nutmeg and baking soda. Beat together the sunflower oil, sugars and eggs until smooth.

2 Stir the flour mixture into the smooth batter. Add the lemon and orange zest, grated carrots, coconut, walnuts, vanilla extract, chopped candied ginger (if using) and soaked raisins with the risidual rum. Stir all the ingredients well to combine. Spoon the mixture into the prepared pan and bake for the time stated or until a skewer inserted into the center of the cake comes out clean.

3 While the cake is baking, make the syrup. Place the sugar in a cup, then add the strained lemon and orange juice. Stir well and continue to stir at intervals. Once the cake is baked, remove it from the oven and immediately pierce it with a skewer several times. Carefully spoon or pour over the citrus syrup then leave the cake to cool before removing it from the pan.

To store This cake keeps fresh for up to 14 days if covered and decorated with icing or wrapped in waxed paper and kept in an airtight container. Suitable for freezing. Allow to thaw overnight.

traditional rich fruit cake

I think it is essential to start with a really good, moist fruit cake for a celebration cake. In my recipe I have included dried dates, prunes and apricots alongside the more commonly used currants and dark and golden raisins: the flavor is more pronounced and a little less sweet. The molasses adds a rich flavor.

This cake improves with keeping: ideally the baked cake should be matured for eight weeks before the event to improve the flavors, and it will keep for up to nine months once decorated with marzipan and icing if stored in a cool, dry place. If, following tradition, you want to reserve the top rich fruit tier of a wedding cake to serve at the first child's christening, wrap the decorated cake in a double layer of waxed paper followed by a double layer of aluminum foil. You can then store it in the freezer until required. The top tier of my wedding cake was frozen for six years before it was thawed and served at my son Marlow's christening. Although this recipe is traditional for a wedding cake, it makes an equally good wedding anniversary, christening or Christmas cake.

ingredients	6-inch	8-inch	10-inch	12-inch
currants	5 oz. (1 cup)	10 oz. (2 cups)	12 oz. (2½ cups)	1 lb. 2 oz. (3⅔ cups)
golden raisins	4 oz. (⅔ cup)	7 oz. (1¼ cups)	11 oz. (1¾ cups)	14 oz. (2½ cups)
dark raisins	4 oz. (⅔ cup)	7 oz. (1¼ cups)	11 oz. (1¾ cups)	14 oz. (2½ cups)
chopped pitted prunes	1½ oz. (⅓ cup)	2½ oz. (⅔ cup)	4 oz. (1 cup)	5½ oz. (1⅓ cups)
chopped dried apricots	1½ oz. (¼ cup)	2½ oz. (½ cup)	4 oz. (⅔ cup)	5½ oz. (1 cup)
chopped pitted dates	1½ oz. (¼ cup)	2½ oz. (½ cup)	4 oz. (⅔ cup)	5½ oz. (1 cup)
chopped natural-color candied cherries	2 oz. (¼ cup)	3½ oz. (½ cup)	5 oz. (⅔ cup)	7 oz. (⅞ cup)
brandy (40% alcohol)	⅓ cup	¾ cup	1 cup	1¼ cups
lemons (juice and zest)	1	2	3	4
oranges (juice and zest)	1	2	3	4
all-purpose flour	6 oz. (1½ cups)	12 oz. (3 cups)	1 lb. 2½ oz. (4¾ cups)	1 lb. 10 oz. (6½ cups)
ground ginger	1 tsp.	2 tsp.	3 tsp.	4 tsp.
ground cinnamon	2 tsp.	4 tsp.	2 tbsp.	2½ tbsp.
ground nutmeg	1½ tsp.	1 tbsp.	1½ tbsp.	2 tbsp.
unsalted butter, softened	5 oz.	9 oz.	13 oz.	1 lb. 2 oz.
light brown sugar	5 oz. (9 tbsp.)	9 oz. (1⅓ cups)	13 oz. (1⅞ cups)	1 lb. 2 oz. (2⅔ cups)
large eggs, beaten	2	4	6	8
molasses	½ tbsp.	1 tbsp.	1½ tbsp.	2 tbsp.
chopped almonds	1 oz. (¼ cup)	2 oz. (½ cup)	3 oz. (¾ cup)	4 oz. (1 cup)
bake convection 250°F				
conventional 275°F	3 hr. 30 min.	4 hr.	5 hr.	5 hr. 30 min.

1 Combine the currants, raisins, prunes, apricots, dates and candied cherries with the brandy and the fresh lemon and orange zest and juice. Leave to absorb for a minimum of 24 hours – ideally 72 hours.

2 Preheat the oven. Have all the ingredients at room temperature. Prepare the cake pan – grease and line with waxed or parchment paper. Sift the flour with the ground ginger, cinnamon and nutmeg. Beat together the butter and sugar until light and fluffy. Beat in the eggs a little at a time, beating well between each addition. Add a few tablespoons of flour to prevent mixture from curdling.

3 Carefully fold the remaining flour into the creamed mixture. Stir in the molasses, then the soaked fruit (reserving the brandy in which it has been soaked) and the chopped nuts.

4 Spoon the mixture into the prepared pan and bake for the time stated. If the top of the cake appears to be browning too quickly, fold a sheet of waxed paper in half, cut a small hole the size of a walnut in the center and carefully place it over the top of the cake. (Make sure you wear oven mitts to do so!)

5 When the cake is cooked, a skewer inserted into the center should come out clean. Leave the cake until it is cold before removing it from the pan. Brush the top with the reserved brandy, then wrap the cake in a double layer of waxed paper and a double layer of aluminum foil to store.

Tip Buy ready-to-eat whole pitted dates, prunes and apricots and snip each piece into 3 using sharp kitchen scissors. This locks the moisture into the fruit. Ready-chopped fruit tends to dry out.

meringue

Meringues are very simple to make and require few ingredients. Because they do not contain any butter or oil, they are a healthier option than a rich cake. They are light and airy and less filling than a more traditional cake, which makes them perfect for a light summer party or cocktail reception or after a rich wedding menu. Toasted chopped hazelnuts can be added to the mixture for extra flavor and texture.

ingredients	10 individual or one 8-inch	20 individual	30 individual	40 individual
large egg whites	2	4	6	8
superfine sugar	4 oz. (½ cup)	8 oz. (1 cup)	12 oz. (1½ cups)	1 lb. (2 cups)
vanilla extract	½ tsp.	½ tsp.	½ tsp.	1 tsp.
vinegar	½ tsp.	½ tsp.	½ tsp.	1 tsp.
finely chopped toasted hazelnuts (optional)	2 oz. (⅓ cup)	3½ oz. (⅔ cup)	5½ oz. (1 cup)	7 oz. (1¼ cups)
bake convection 250°F conventional 300°F		30 minutes, then 4 hours		

1 Preheat the oven. Have all the ingredients at room temperature. Place the egg whites in a clean, grease-free bowl and beat on high speed until the egg white reaches the stiff peak stage. It should not be dry. Add the sugar 1 tablespoon at a time until the mixture is thick and glossy. Whisk in the vanilla extract and vinegar. If using hazelnuts, carefully fold them in at this stage.

2 For individual meringues, heap a tablespoon of the mixture onto a baking sheet lined with parchment paper and hollow out the center of each with the back of a metal spoon. For 1 large meringue, draw an 8-inch circle on the reverse of parchment paper with a pencil. Use this as a guide for spreading the mixture. Hollow out the center with the back of a metal spoon.

3 Place the meringues in the oven and immediately reduce the heat to 225°F on a convection oven or 275°F on a conventional oven. After 30 minutes, turn the oven off and leave the meringues to dry out in the heat of the oven — ideally overnight but for at least 4 hours — until they are completely cold.

To serve When you are ready to serve the meringues, they can be lined with chocolate and, once set, filled with cream. Once filled, they should be eaten within 4 hours to prevent the meringue becoming soggy. Unfilled meringues can be stored in an airtight container until required for up to 4 weeks.

cookies

Hand-decorated cookies can be an effective way to extend the theme of a party. Personalize cookies for children by piping their names on them and present them in clear cellophane tied with a ribbon, or decorate them as butterflies with bright-colored icing to make pretty table decorations.

spiced cookies

Makes approximately 60 small cookies or 20 large cookies

you will need

2¼ cups self-rising flour

½ tsp. ground cinnamon

½ tsp. ground nutmeg

¼ tsp. ground ginger

4½ oz. unsalted butter

¾ cup light brown sugar

2 oz. (½ cup) ground almonds

½ tsp. almond extract

1 large egg, beaten

to bake

convection 325°F

conventional 350°F

10 minutes small cookies

14 minutes large cookies

1 Preheat the oven. Line a baking sheet with parchment paper. Sift flour, cinnamon, nutmeg and ginger into a bowl. Cut butter into small pieces and rub into the flour until the mixture resembles fine breadcrumbs. Stir in the sugar, ground almonds and almond extract. Stir in the beaten egg to bind the dough together and knead into a neat ball. Gather up the dough and wrap in plastic wrap. Place in the refrigerator to rest for 20 minutes.

2 Roll out the dough on a lightly floured board to a depth of ¼ inch for small cookies or ½ inch for large cookies. Place the cookies on the prepared baking sheet and bake in the oven until they are golden around the edges. Carefully lift the cookies onto a wire rack and allow them to cool completely before decorating them.

lemon and almond cookies

Makes approximately 60 small or 20 large cookies

you will need

6 oz. unsalted butter

¾ cup superfine sugar

1 large egg, beaten

2⅔ cups self-rising flour, sifted

zest of 2 fresh lemons

2 oz. (½ cup) ground almonds

½ tsp. almond extract

to bake

convection 325°F

conventional 350°F

8 minutes small cookies

12 minutes large cookies

1 Preheat the oven. Have all the ingredients at room temperature. Line a baking sheet with parchment paper. Beat together the softened butter and sugar until light and fluffy. Add half the beaten egg and whisk. Stir in the sifted flour, lemon zest, almonds, almond extract and the remainder of the egg to form a dough. Wrap in plastic wrap and place in the refrigerator to rest for 20 minutes.

2 Roll out the dough onto a lightly floured board to ¼ inch thickness for small cookies, ½ inch for larger cookies. Place cookies on the lined baking sheet and bake until golden around the edges. Carefully lift the cookies onto a wire rack and allow them to cool before decorating them.

buttercream

Buttercream is a combination of softened unsalted butter and confectioners' sugar. The basic mixture can be combined with other flavors: these lemon curd, espresso and chocolate ganache versions are particularly good.

you will need

9 oz. unsalted butter, softened

4 cups confectioners' sugar

1 tsp. vanilla extract

yields about 3 cups

Beat the softened butter for 2 minutes using an electric mixer. Sift in the confectioners' sugar and beat slowly at first. Add the vanilla extract then, with the mixer on full speed, whip until the buttercream is very light and fluffy.

lemon curd buttercream

The luscious lemon cake (see page 15) is so fresh and light it really needs little accompaniment, but a light, creamy lemon buttercream complements it beautifully. Simply stir 10 oz. of lemon curd into 1 recipe of buttercream.

espresso buttercream

The deliciously sophisticated coffee and walnut cake (see page 14) really benefits from the inclusion of a layer of espresso buttercream. Pour ⅓ cup freshly boiled water over 2 heaped tablespoons of ground coffee. Allow to infuse, then filter the liquid espresso. Add 2 tablespoons of cooled espresso – 3 for a more pronounced flavor – to 1 recipe of buttercream.

chocolate ganache buttercream

Chocolate ganache is a blend of boiled cream and chocolate. It has a smooth, rich, velvety texture that literally melts in the mouth. Mixed with buttercream it becomes a wonderfully decadent filling or frosting for the chocolate truffle torte (see page 13).

you will need

6 oz. dark chocolate
(70% cocoa solids),
broken into pieces
½ cup cream
1 recipe of buttercream

yields about 4¼ cups

Place the chocolate pieces in a clean dry bowl. Bring the cream to the boil, remove from the heat and pour over the chocolate. Stir with a wooden spoon until the chocolate is melted and the ganache is smooth and glossy. Allow the chocolate ganache to cool for 15 minutes before beating it into the buttercream. Store any excess buttercream in the refrigerator for up to 2 weeks.

size of cake	6-inch	8-inch	10-inch	12-inch
to sandwich 2 halves	½ recipe	1 recipe	1½ recipes	2 recipes
to cover top and sides	½ recipe	1 recipe	1½ recipes	2 recipes

alternative flavors

Lime buttercream Add the zest of 1 lime and 3 drops of lime oil to 1 recipe of plain vanilla buttercream. This buttercream works well with the luscious lemon cake – particularly for individual ganache bites.

Orange buttercream Add the zest of 1 medium orange to 1 recipe of plain vanilla buttercream. This buttercream can be used to sandwich and cover layers of the moist carrot cake (see pages 16–7).

Toasted pecan buttercream Toast 2 oz. pecans under a broiler, chop coarsely and add to 1 recipe of chocolate ganache buttercream. This is a particularly good option for cakes that are not being dressed with fresh fruit.

covering a cake with marzipan

One question I am asked more than any other is: 'Do I have to use marzipan?' We seem to be divided into lovers or loathers of this luxurious almond paste. I definitely fall into the first category – as a student I would bake my own fruit cakes with an additional layer of marzipan in the center. In fact, apart from its taste, marzipan plays a threefold role as a covering for a fruit cake: firstly, it protects the baked cake, locking in moisture as the almonds have a rich oil content; secondly, it adds form and stability – especially if the cake is destined to become a tiered cake; thirdly, it provides a good clean base for the icing, which prevents the color of the cake bleeding through. For multitiered cakes I recommend it as essential; however, you could cover a single-tier cake with a double layer of fondant instead if you wish.

for fondant

How you cover a cake with marzipan depends on whether you are going to be using fondant or royal icing. For fondant, the marzipan is rolled out and smoothed over the cake in one piece to create softly rounded edges.

you will need

cake

thin board the same size as the cake

pastry brush

boiled, strained apricot jam

marzipan

confectioners' sugar

rolling pin

smoother

turntable or bowl

sharp knife

1 Place the cooled baked cake upside down on a thin cake board the same size as the cake and brush liberally with boiled, strained apricot jam. Knead the marzipan until smooth and pliable. Dust the work surface lightly with confectioners' sugar and roll the marzipan evenly into a size large enough to cover the top and sides of the cake, allowing for surplus (use string to measure). The marzipan should be approximately ¼ inch thick. Carefully lift the marzipan onto the cake.

2 Smooth the top and sides of the cake using your hands and a smoother. Trim off the majority of the excess marzipan.

3 Lift the cake onto a turntable or upturned bowl and neatly trim the final excess marzipan using a sharp knife and keeping it flush with the bottom of the board.

size of cake	6-inch ●	6-inch ■	8-inch ●	8-inch ■	9-inch ●	9-inch ■	10-inch ●	10-inch ■	12-inch ●	12-inch ■	14-inch ●	14-inch ■	16-inch ●	16-inch ■
recipe	1 lb. 5 oz.	1 lb. 10 oz.	1 lb. 12 oz.	2 lb. 4 oz.	2 lb. 4 oz.	2 lb. 12 oz.	2 lb. 12 oz.	3 lb. 8 oz.	3 lb. 8 oz.	4 lb. 8 oz.	5 lb.		5 lb. 13 oz.	6 lb. 4 oz.	6 lb. 10 oz.

for royal icing

Cakes covered with royal icing should have sharp, clean, angular edges, and so the marzipan needs to be rolled out and applied as separate pieces. This method is more time consuming, but the finished result is well worth it.

you will need

cake
thick board 3 inches larger than the cake
pastry brush
boiled, strained apricot jam
marzipan
confectioners' sugar
rolling pin
sharp knife

Tip If the cake is very domed, slice the peak off to level the surface. You can roll a thin sausage of marzipan and use this to build up any uneven edges around the base of the cake once it has been turned upside down.

2

1 Place the cooled baked cake upside down in the center of the baseboard and brush liberally with boiled, strained apricot jam. Knead the marzipan until smooth and pliable. Dust the work surface lightly with confectioners' sugar and roll the marzipan evenly into a size large enough to cut out the top and sides separately and accurately (use string or a ruler to measure). The marzipan should be approximately ¼ inch thick.

2 Using both hands, carefully lift the marzipan onto the cake. Fix the top in position first, then apply each of the sides in turn. Trim any excess with a sharp knife. Allow to set overnight before applying the royal icing.

covering a cake with fondant

Fondant is a wonderful invention. Rolled out like marzipan and smoothed over the cake, this sweet paste creates a fast, clean, smooth finish with gently curved edges. It provides a very good base for additional decoration or looks clean, classical and contemporary simply adorned with fresh flowers. It is soft and pliable to apply; sets firm but not rock hard; cuts beautifully and has a shelf life of one year. However, It does not like to get wet – moisture will dissolve the sugar leaving craters, so keep all utensils clean and thoroughly dry.

you will need

marzipan-covered cake placed on a thin board of the same size

thick board 3 inches larger than the cake

pastry brush

confectioners' sugar

fondant

rolling pin

smoother

sharp knife

brandy or cooled boiled water

turntable or bowl

metal spatula

small quantity of royal icing

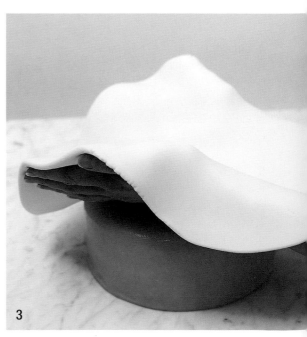

1 Brush the thick baseboard with cooled boiled water. Dust the work surface lightly with confectioners' sugar (too much will dry the icing) and knead the fondant until smooth and pliable. Evenly roll the icing to the correct size – large enough to cover the baseboard and approximately ⅛ inch thick. Carefully place the icing over the board and use a smoother to finish. Holding the board in one hand, use a sharp knife to cut away the excess, keeping the knife flush with the side of the board. Set aside to set (ideally overnight)

2 Brush the marzipan-covered cake with brandy or cooled boiled water. This acts as a good antiseptic seal between the marzipan and fondant as well as being an adhesive.

3 Dust the work surface lightly with confectioners' sugar and knead the fondant until smooth and pliable. Evenly roll the fondant into a size large enough to cover the top and sides of the cake, allowing for surplus (use string to measure). It should be approximately ¼ inch thick. Carefully lift the icing onto the marzipan-covered cake.

guide to quantities to cover cakes with fondant

● round cake   ■ square cake

size of cake	6-inch ●	6-inch ■	8-inch ●	8-inch ■	9-inch ●	9-inch ■	10-inch ●	10-inch ■	12-inch ●	12-inch ■	14-inch ●	14-inch ■	16-inch ●	16-inch ■
quantity	1 lb. 10 oz.	1 lb. 14 oz.	2 lb. 4 oz.	2 lb. 12 oz.	2 lb. 12 oz.	3 lb. 8 oz.	3 lb. 8 oz.	4 lb.	4 lb. 10 oz.	5 lb. 3 oz.	6 lb.	6 lb. 10 oz.	7 lb. 3 oz.	7 lb. 11 oz.

guide to quantities to cover cake boards with fondant

size of cake	6-inch ●	6-inch ■	8-inch ●	8-inch ■	9-inch ●	9-inch ■	10-inch ●	10-inch ■	12-inch ●	12-inch ■	14-inch ●	14-inch ■	16-inch ●	16-inch ■
quantity	9 oz.	12 oz.	1 lb. 3½ oz.	1 lb. 7 oz.	1 lb. 8 oz.	1 lb. 10 oz.	1 lb. 12 oz.	1 lb. 13 oz.	1 lb. 13 oz.	1 lb. 14 oz.	2 lb.	2 lb. 2 oz.	2 lb. 2 oz.	2 lb. 4 oz.

4   5   6

7

4 Smooth the top and sides with your hands, carefully pressing the fondant against the cake. Be careful not to drag the icing down the sides of the cake as this will cause it to crack and tear.

5 Use a smoother to give the cake a professional, clean finish and prick any air bubbles with a pin. Trim the majority of the excess fondant away from the cake.

6 Lift the cake onto a turntable or upturned bowl and neatly trim away all the excess fondant using a sharp knife, keeping the knife flush with the bottom of the board.

7 Slide a metal spatula carefully underneath the cake and board and lift from underneath using both hands. Put a dab of royal icing on the pre-lined baseboard and carefully set the cake in position on top.

royal icing

Royal icing is traditional and is staging a comeback! Made from fresh egg white and confectioners' sugar, royal icing is a sweet paste that is lathered onto the cake and allowed to set. Once made, royal icing will keep fresh in an airtight container for up to 7 days. It will separate if left for longer than 24 hours and should be rewhisked before using.

for piping:
1 large egg white
3 cups confectioners' sugar, sifted
juice of ½ lemon, strained

yields about 1 cup

Place the egg white into a clean, grease-free bowl and beat until it forms very soft peaks. Add the confectioners' sugar and beat slowly at first until all the sugar is incorporated, then on full speed for 1 minute. Add the lemon juice and beat for another minute.

for covering:
For icing to be used for covering a cake, add 1 teaspoon of glycerine per 1 lb. icing and omit the lemon juice. This will allow the icing to be cut without it splintering.

Tip Reconstituted albumen powder can be substituted for fresh egg white and is available from specialist cake suppliers. It should be used according to the manufacturer's instructions, but the ratio is generally 1 oz. albumen powder and ⅓ cup water to 2 lb. confectioners' sugar.

guide to quantities to cover cakes with royal icing

● round cake   ■ square cake

size of cake	6-inch ●	6-inch ■	8-inch ●	8-inch ■	9-inch ●	9-inch ■	10-inch ●	10-inch ■	12-inch ●	12-inch ■	14-inch ●	14-inch ■	16-inch ●	16-inch ■
quantity	1 lb. 12 oz.	2 lb. 4 oz.	2 lb. 4 oz.	2 lb. 12 oz.	2 lb. 12 oz.	3 lb. 8 oz.	3 lb. 8 oz.	3 lb. 14 oz.	4 lb. 8 oz.	5 lb.	5 lb. 8 oz.	6 lb.	6 lb. 10 oz.	7 lb. 3 oz.

flooding icing

For flooding icing, thin the royal icing down with drops of egg white or water. Egg white will make the finished run-out stronger but the icing may take longer to dry. Thinning the icing with water will enable it to dry quicker but it will be less strong. Add additional liquid a drop at a time to the royal icing and stir gently. Do not beat the icing at this stage as you will incorporate too much air and bubbles will appear in the run-outs. To judge the amount of water to add, swirl a knife in the bowl and count steadily to 10 as the ripples subside.

1

covering a cake with royal icing

Covering a cake with royal icing is a much more laborious technique than using fondant, as several coats are required to build the icing up to the desired thickness. It sets very firm and is somewhat brittle to slice, but the finished icing has a wonderfully sweet flavor and a clean, architectural finish that is perfect for particular designs, for example the 1950s chic and Art Deco cakes (see pages 118–9 and 134–5 respectively).

you will need

marzipan-covered cake placed on a thick board 3 inches larger than cake

fresh royal icing

metal spatula

top and side scrapers

sharp knife

1 Prepare the royal icing. Use a metal spatula to apply the royal icing liberally onto one of the sides of the marzipan-covered cake in a patting motion to expel any air bubbles from the icing.

2 Hold a side scraper at a 45-degree angle to the cake and steadily and purposefully pull it towards you. Use a sharp knife in a downward motion to remove the excess icing from the 2 side ends and top edge. Repeat on the opposite side. Allow the icing to set for at least 8 hours before repeating the process on the other 2 sides.

2

4

3 Spread the royal icing liberally on the top of the cake. Using a long scraper and holding the ends away from the cake, carefully pull the scraper at an angle of 45 degrees across the top of the cake towards you. Use a sharp knife to trim the edges. Allow to set for 8 hours in a warm, dry environment. Repeat steps 1–3 until all sides and the top of the cake have received 3 coats.

4 To cover the board, spread the royal icing onto each side in turn and, holding a side scraper at a 45-degree angle to the board, carefully pull it towards you. Clean the edges with a sharp knife.

piping icing

All of the iced designs in this book are created using royal icing – a blend of egg white and confectioners' sugar. The icing is whipped until it is glossy, at which point it will dry, harden and set on exposure to air. Royal icing can be prepared from fresh egg white (see page 28) or commercially produced dried albumen powder and is versatile in that it can be used for covering cakes, adding fine detail or can be thinned down for flooding run-outs. Once the royal icing is prepared, it is essential to keep it covered, either with a clean damp cloth or in an airtight container.

making a pastry bag

Pastry or decorating bags are made from waxed or parchment paper triangles. The larger the triangle, the larger the decorating bag. I like to make various sizes – smaller ones for flooding lots of different colors and larger ones for piping single colors onto a number of tiers.

1 Fold a 12- to 18-inch square of waxed paper in half diagonally to make 2 triangles and cut the paper in half along the crease. Place the paper on the table with the tip of the triangle facing you and bring the underside of the left point to the right of center and hold with your thumb and forefinger.

2 Bring the right hand point up, over and round to the back to meet the center.

3 Carefully fold the corner of the paper over to secure the bag, as shown.

icing techniques

All the iced cakes in this book have been hand decorated using a pastry bag filled with a tip and royal icing. Snip the end of the pastry bag and drop in a tip. For flooding, the pastry bag has no tip – the end is snipped once the bag is filled. Hold the bag and fill two-thirds full with royal icing. Fold the highest point of the bag over and tuck the sides in to prevent the icing oozing out. Hold the bag in your hand between your second and third fingers and use your thumb on the top of the bag to exert pressure to force the icing out in a controlled manner.

1 No. 1.5 tip – small plain tip
Used for small pearls, vanity fair, tiffany pearl ribbon and outlines for all run-outs.

2 No. 2 tip – medium plain tip
Used for brush embroidery, smaller pearls, Fabergé and fleur-de-lis designs.

3 No. 3 tip – large plain tip
Used for bead trails around the base of cakes and for candy stripe design.

4 No. 5 tip – star tip
Used for star trails around the base of the cakes, individual stars and scroll hearts.

glazing

There are a number of lusters and edible gels available, which can dramatically enhance elements of a hand-iced cake. Pearls can be brought to life with edible gel to maintain a dewy appearance and whole sections of icing can be brushed with lusters mixed with alcohol dipping solution for an authentic sparkle.

edible gel

Made from a sugar glucose solution, edible gel can be brushed neatly onto set icing to create an instant wet look. The gel remains slightly tacky even when set so be careful when handling the finished cake.

edible gel mixed with lusters

For the fleur-de-lis (see pages 126–7) and the Fabergé cake (see pages 130–1), shown here, I have mixed ½ teaspoon of topaz luster with 1 teaspoon of edible gel to create a paste. This is then brushed onto the pearls for an authentic dewy pearly shine. Various colors of lusters are available including ruby, sapphire, jade, copper and gold.

lusters mixed with alcohol dipping solution

Lusters can also be dissolved in alcohol and brushed onto set icing as on vanity fair and caramel tiara cakes (see pages 132–3 and 138). The alcohol allows you to brush the luster onto the pearls but then evaporates, leaving a matte-sheen appearance. Be careful, as the luster will brush off or mark the cake if it is touched.

individual cake stands

Small cakes presented on a stand are becoming increasingly popular and are an effective way to create height and drama for more intimate celebrations. Here I have shown how to make two display stands: an iced one for individual iced cakes and a chocolate one to present chocolate cakes or pavlova. Stands can be made in many shapes and sizes – round, square and hexagonal are the most practical. Decide on the number and size of tiers and calculate the quantity of individual cakes you will need using the table below.

iced stand

The individual iced cakes shown in this book (see pages 49, 108–9 and 140–3) are presented on iced stands. I like to coordinate the color of the icing on the stand and the ribbon with the mini cakes.

you will need

confectioners' sugar
fondant
rolling pin
cake boards
pastry brush
smoother
glue stick
⅝-inch width ribbon, sufficient length to edge boards and wrap around central columns
polystyrene colums
royal icing

Tip Make your top tier no smaller than 8-inch diameter. This will allow the tier below to have an acceptable size polystyrene column to support the top tier while providing sufficient space to display the cakes.

1 Lightly dust a work surface with confectioners' sugar. Knead the fondant until pliable and smooth. Working on one board at a time, roll out paste large enough to cover the board to ¼ inch thick.

2 Brush the board with cold water then lift the icing over the board. Smooth the icing then, holding the knife against the board, cut away the excess icing.

3 Rub glue stick around the edge of the board and attach a length of ⅝-inch width ribbon. Rub glue over the polystyrene column and wrap the ribbon around it, starting at the bottom edge and working your way up, carefully overlapping as you go until you reach the top edge. Glue the final piece into position.

4 Fix the central columns into position with royal icing on each tier and allow to set overnight. Assemble the stand by securing the tiers together with royal icing.

size of board	round stand		square stand		hexagonal stand	
	2-inch diam cakes/pavlova	1½-inch ganache bites	2-inch diam cakes/pavlova	1½-inch diam ganache bites	2-inch diam cakes/pavlova	1½-inch ganache bites
8 inches	5	7	8	10	6	9
10 inches	9	12	12	15	8	11
12 inches	10	15	12	20	11	15
14 inches	12	18	16	24	12	18
16 inches	14	20	20	28	14	20
18 inches	17	24	24	30	16	24

chocolate-covered stand

Chocolate stands can be painted with white or dark chocolate: white chocolate creates the right look for a wedding cake, while dark chocolate stands are suitable for cocktail and dinner parties. Coating chocolate, though inappropriate for use in recipes, is ideal for covering cake stands: it is less expensive than real chocolate and sets very quickly once melted and painted onto the stand as it contains a high percentage of vegetable fat.

you will need

glue stick or royal icing

3-inch high polystyrene columns

cake boards

coating chocolate

2-inch paintbrush

edible spray varnish (optional)

1 Glue or ice the polystyrene columns onto the center of each board, except the top one. Melt the coating chocolate in a bowl over simmering water or in a microwave. Using a 2-inch paintbrush, paint the chocolate over the board and up the sides of the polystyrene.

2 Glue or ice the stand together ensuring each tier is centrally positioned. For added protection, spray the stand with an edible spray varnish. Store the stand in a cool, dry place out of direct sunlight or heat until required.

Tip Once the polystyrene columns are positioned, the stand should still have at least a 3-inch space all around to hold the cakes comfortably.

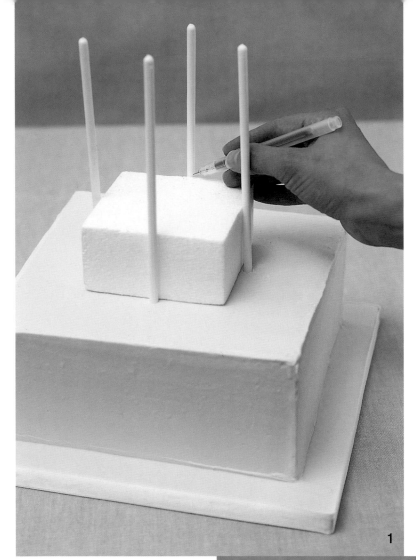

blocking a cake

Blocking a cake with fresh flowers or fruit is a stunning way to present it and creates an illusion that each tier is suspended on a bed of fruit or flowers. Blocking is also one of the most stable methods of stacking tiers. The polystyrene blocks provide surface-area stability for the tier above and also a base for wired flowers.

1 Place the polystyrene blocks in the center of the 2 largest tiers. Insert a dowel at the center point of each side of the block, making sure they are straight and pushed down to the boards. Mark each dowel where it meets the top of the block.

2 Remove dowels and line up on a table. Using a ruler and pen, re-mark each one to the highest point. (This will ensure the cake is level and supported when the dowels are reinserted and the next tier is stacked into position.) Cut each dowel to the new mark. Replace the dowels in each cake so they are flush with the top of the polystyrene blocks.

3 Using both hands, gently lift the middle tier, carefully positioning it on the block of the base one until it is central, stable and even. Repeat with the top tier. Edge each board with ribbon, securing it at the back of the cake with glue.

1

you will need

3 cake tiers, covered with marzipan and royal icing and placed centrally on thick boards 3 inches larger than each cake, covered with royal icing

2 polystyrene blocks, 2 inches deep and 4 inches smaller than the medium and largest cake tier

8 dowels

pen

ruler

sharp heavy-duty scissors or a small hacksaw

⅝-inch width ribbon to edge each board

glue stick

Tip Make sure that you scale the polystyrene blocks with the size of the tiers to maintain stability and to allow sufficient space for the flowers or fruit.

3

stacking a cake

Stacking is a preferred American way to present a finished wedding cake. The tiers, which are stacked either centrally over each other or offset, are supported with hidden boards and dowels. The overall height of a stacked cake is less than other tiered cakes. For a grander effect, you can increase the number of tiers, including some false upper tiers if necessary.

1 Spread a small amount of royal icing on the larger baseboard and fix the smaller board in position by pressing it firmly. Place a small amount of royal icing on the top baseboard and position the base cake tier centrally on top. Push 6 dowels randomly into the center of the cake, making sure their line does not fall outside the size of the tier to be stacked above. Use a pen to mark each dowel at the point it surfaces from the cake.

2 Remove the dowels and line them up on a table. Find the average mark and, using a ruler and pen, mark each of the dowels at the same point. (This will ensure the cake is level and supported when the dowels are reinserted and the next tier is placed into position.) Cut each dowel to the new mark using heavy-duty scissors or a small hacksaw. Check each dowel is the correct length before reinserting them all into the cake as they will be very difficult to remove again. Once the dowels are pushed right into the cake, spread a small amount of royal icing on the center of the cake with a metal spatula.

3 Use both hands to gently hold the next tier and carefully position it onto the base cake. Repeat step 2 with another 6 dowels before placing the top tier into position. Cut lengths of 1-inch width ribbon to fix around each tier. Secure these in place with a dab of royal icing at the back and base of each tier. Edge each of the 2 iced baseboards with ⅝-inch width ribbon, using glue stick to secure it in position. Ensure that the joins are at the back of the cakes.

Tip Leave the cakes for 24 hours after covering them with marzipan and icing before attempting to stack them. This allows time for the marzipan and icing to harden and set so that you will be able to handle the tiers without the icing cracking or dimpling.

you will need

3 cake tiers covered with marzipan and icing and placed on thin boards of the same size and shape

2 baseboards, 3 inches and 6 inches larger than base tier, covered with icing

royal icing

12 dowels

pen

ruler

sharp heavy-duty scissors or a small hacksaw

metal spatula

1-inch width ribbon to fix around each tier

⅝-inch width ribbon to edge baseboards

glue stick

1

2

3

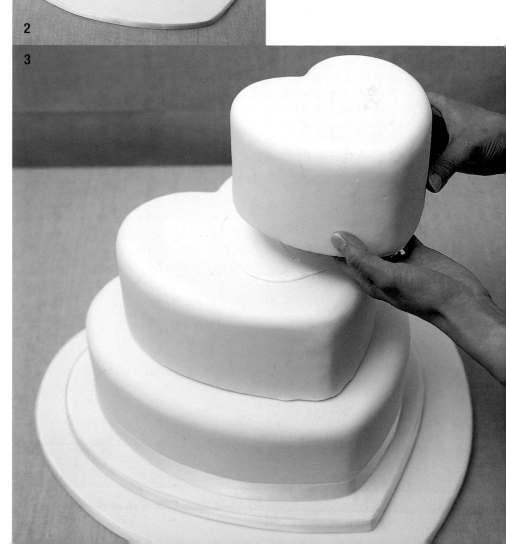

using pillars to separate tiers

Separating tiers with pillars is a traditional way to add dramatic height and grandeur to a cake and the space created between the tiers can be dressed with fresh, sugar or silk flowers. Pillars are available in many heights, colors and finishes – dowels placed inside the pillars carry all the weight of the tiers. With very large or heavy tiers, increase the number of pillars – the grid supplied (see page 146) has markings for 3, 4, 6 or 8 pillars on each tier.

you will need

3 cake tiers, each covered with marzipan and fondant

4 thick boards, 3 inches larger than each cake tier and one 6 inches larger than the base tier, covered with fondant

grid template (see page 146)

scribe

6 dowels

6 (3½-inch) pillars

ruler

pen

sharp heavy-duty scissors or a small hacksaw

⅝-inch width ribbon to edge each baseboard

glue stick

1 Start with all cakes positioned on boards and the base tier on the largest baseboard. Place the grid template centrally over the largest tier and use a scribe to mark 3 points along guide C.

2 Insert a dowel into each of the marked points and drop a pillar over the top. Place a ruler across 2 of the pillars and mark the dowels at the top of the pillars with a pen. Move the ruler around to between one of these pillars and the third one and finally between this pillar and the first one marking the rods each time. Remove the pillars and dowels from the cake.

3 Line the dowels up and use a ruler to measure and a pen to mark the average point. This will ensure the cake is level and supported when the dowels are replaced and the next tier is stacked into position. Cut each dowel to the new mark using heavy-duty scissors or a small hacksaw. Replace the dowels into cake and position a pillar carefully over each one.

4 Repeat the above with the middle tier. Edge each of the iced baseboards with ⅝-inch width ribbon and secure in position with glue stick, ensuring that the point at which the ribbon joins on each of the boards is facing the back of the cake. Finally, stack the tiers, making sure they are level, stable and centered.

stacking tiers with a central column

Separating cake tiers with a central column gives a contemporary, uncluttered look and wrapping the column in a contrasting or complementary ribbon creates a dramatic or more subtle effect. It's not necessary to add finishing touches between the tiers so this technique is popular for designs that reach or cover the top of each tier so that they can be clearly seen.

you will need

3 cake tiers, covered with marzipan and fondant

3 baseboards, 3 inches larger than each cake tier, covered with fondant

grid template (see page 146)

scribe

dowels

ruler

pen

sharp heavy-duty scissors or a small hacksaw

2 polystyrene blocks, 2 inches deep and 4 inches smaller than the medium and largest cake tier

1-inch width ribbon to edge each polystyrene block

glue stick

2 thin boards of the same size and shape as the polystyrene blocks

royal icing

⅝-inch width ribbon to edge each baseboard

Tip As this technique is less stable than other methods for tiering cakes, restrict its use to a maximum of 4 tiers.

1 Start with cakes positioned on boards. Place the grid template centrally over the largest cake and mark the center point onto the cake with a scribe.

2 Insert a dowel into the center of the largest cake, making sure it is straight and pushed down to the cake board. Mark the dowel with a pen at the point where it surfaces from the top of the cake. Remove the dowel and line it up with 4 others. Use a ruler and pen to mark each dowel to the measured point. (This will ensure that the cake is level and supported when the dowels are replaced and the next tier is stacked into position.)

3 Cut each dowel to the new mark using heavy-duty scissors or a small hacksaw. Push the dowels into the cake, keeping them within the diameter of the central column. Cover the largest polystyrene block with 1-inch width ribbon, wrapping it around the block several times to ensure the polystyrene is covered and securing it in position with glue stick. Glue the block to a thin board the same size and shape as (to prevent the dowels pushing through the polystyrene under the weight of the cake). Spread a small amount of royal icing in the center of the cake.

4 Carefully position the polystyrene block onto the cake (board side facing down), ensuring that the center of the block is over the central dowel. Repeat with the middle tier and allow both tiers to set for 30 minutes before assembling them.

Edge each of the baseboards with ⅝-inch width ribbon and secure it in position with glue stick, ensuring that the ribbon joins on each of the boards and polystyrene blocks is facing the back of the cake. Finally, carefully stack the tiers.

finishing touches

Deciding on suitable decoration for your cake can be a dilemma. The design of cake you choose should befit the occasion and should also be a reflection of the personality of the recipient. Once you have selected a basic design, you can choose to dress the finished cake in many ways.

Fresh flowers are one of my favorite ways to dress a cake, as you will see throughout this book. The effect is instantaneous and dramatic and the scent will enhance any occasion. Fresh flowers can be blocked between tiers without the concern of icing shattering or being damaged and they can complement the tone of the occasion. Fresh flowers can be set into a dome of oasis for protection or simply hand tied. Remove fresh flowers before cutting and serving the cake, as, unless specified, they are not edible.

Silk flowers can safely be packed between tiers, and are an effective alternative to fresh flowers, although they do tend to be more expensive.

Sugar flowers, like silk ones, have the advantage that they can last forever, making ideal keepsakes. However, they are extremely fragile and brittle so reserve them for dressing between tall pillars or fixing to the outside of the cake, as on the cascading lily cake (see pages 120–1).

Fresh fruit adds instant color and has a great affinity with chocolate – a combination of summer or autumn berries can be piled onto the top of a cake or chocolate-dipped strawberries studded over a chocolate helter-skelter (see pages 136–7).

Sugar butterflies (see pages 124–5) are an effective finishing touch. They can be a mass of bright colors or in soft pastels with shimmers of glitter. Alternatively, look for a variety of silk or lace wired butterflies, doves or dragonflies.

Cute cake toppers add height and humor to a cake. At Little Venice Cake Company we make characters from clay based on photographs supplied by our clients. They are a custom-made keepsake and a lovely reminder of the special occasion. You can also create edible characters from modeling paste or chocolate plastic.

iced cakes

working with icing

This chapter introduces several piping techniques and styles to build up your cake-decorating repertoire. With royal icing, a pastry bag and a plain tip you can create precision-perfect pearls, ribbon loops, funky candy stripes or delicate lace embroidery. Once you've mastered these techniques, use them to create your own designs.

tiffany pearl ribbon

you will need

6-inch and 10-inch square cakes covered with marzipan and fondant

13-inch baseboard covered with fondant

pastry bags

no. 1.5 tip

royal icing

½-inch width ribbon to fix around each tier

glue stick (to fix ribbon around baseboard)

⅝-inch width ribbon to edge baseboard

fresh flowers to dress

For a more intimate celebration or wedding anniversary, I like this combination of a 6-inch cake offset to the back of a 10-inch square cake positioned on a 13-inch board. It looks particularly sophisticated with an elegant bunch of burgundy arum lilies. Transform this design by altering the spacing, size and color of the pearls.

2

1 Stack cakes following instructions on page 35, positioning the bottom tier towards the back corner of the covered board. Fill a pastry bag with a no. 1.5 piping tip and fresh royal icing. Fix the ribbon around the base of each tier and around the baseboard. Beginning with the top tier, pipe the first row of pearls just above the ribbon, ensuring that they are evenly positioned.

2 Working on one side of the cake at a time, move the pastry bag upwards a little and pipe the second row of pearls in between the first row. Repeat until you have six rows of pearls on each side of the top tier, then repeat on the bottom tier. Finally dress the top of the cake with fresh flowers.

full tiffany pearl

you will need

cake covered with marzipan and
fondant and placed centrally on a
baseboard 3 inches larger

pastry bag

no. 2 tip

royal icing

½-inch width ribbon for the cake

glue stick

⅝-inch width ribbon to edge
the board

fresh flowers to dress

Here the entire side of the cake is precision piped with pearls. I like to use a slightly larger tip and find the whole process rather therapeutic. If you are working on several tiers, always keep one finished tier beside you to ensure that you maintain continuity of the pearl size and spacing. If this is your first attempt, try white pearls on a white cake so that they can be easily removed if you make a mistake.

1 Fill a pastry bag with a no. 2 piping tip and fresh royal icing. Fix the narrower ribbon around the base of the cake and secure with a dab of royal icing. Glue the wider ribbon around the board. Pipe the first row of pearls just above the ribbon, ensuring that they are evenly positioned and work around the whole tier. (If there is more than one tier, start on the top one.)

2 Moving up a little, pipe the second row of pearls in between the first row. Complete the whole row before moving on to the next. (It may be a good idea to position the cake on a turntable for this.) Repeat until you reach the top of the cake. Dress the cake with fresh flowers.

cascading pearls

you will need

3-tier cake covered with marzipan and fondant and placed on boards the same size as each tier

baseboard 2 inches larger than bottom tier, covered with icing

pastry bags

no. 3 tip

royal icing

½-inch width ribbon to fix around each tier

paintbrush

1 tsp. topaz luster

2 tsp. clear piping gel

2 (2-inch) polystyrene blocks, 4 inches smaller than the size of the middle and bottom tiers

fresh wired flowers

glue stick

⅝-inch width ribbon to edge the baseboard

This design is very simple for the novice cake decorator as there is no pre-marking or structure to follow. Each of the tiers is placed on a board the same size as the cake it supports, so handle the tiers with care, holding them from underneath. I find this cake works particularly well if partnered with strong solid flowers; here I have blocked the cake with a mixture of 'Ecstasy' and 'Aqua' roses, burgundy ranunculus and gloriosa lilies.

1 Begin with cakes covered and the bottom tier positioned on the covered board. Fill a pastry bag with a no. 3 piping tip and fresh royal icing. Fix narrower ribbon around the base of each tier. Begin piping the pearls randomly on each tier, concentrating at the base and making fewer as you move up the side of the cake as shown. Each pearl should have a diameter of approximately ½ inch. Use a clean, damp paintbrush to remove the point of each pearl. Repeat on all tiers.

2 Once the icing is dry, the pearls can be brushed with a glaze – use topaz luster mixed with clear piping gel. Block each tier as shown on page 34 and stud with fresh, wired flowers (see page 53) before stacking the tiers. Finally, glue the wider ribbon around the baseboard.

modern cascading pearls

This elegant square wedding cake has been covered in ivory fondant to create smooth soft edges, then hand decorated with cascading pearls in white royal icing. I have included a border of pearls around the base for a special finishing touch. The pearls have been glazed with a clear edible gel so they glisten and the finished cake dressed with fresh white lilies.

3-tier caramel ribbon loops

Individual hand-iced ribbon loops can also be used to decorate a stacked, tiered cake. For this cake I have used a combination of white, ivory and caramel loops on an ivory-covered cake. The tiers are stacked and surrounded with 1-inch width gold ribbon before the loops are fixed into position at an angle around each tier with royal icing. I have presented this cake on a contemporary square board.

ribbon loops

you will need

2-inch cube cakes covered with marzipan and fondant

½-inch width ribbon for fixing around each cake

colored and white royal icing

pastry bags

no. 3 tips

heavy-duty waxed paper

iced boards

⅝-inch width ribbon for edging boards

glue stick

3-inch high polystyrene columns

You can create extremely versatile designs using fresh royal icing and a plain tip. This cake is a novel display of individual cakes, each dressed with hand-piped, royal-iced ribbon loops.

1 Attach a length of ½-inch ribbon around each cake, securing it with royal icing at the back of the cake. Using a pastry bag fitted with a no. 3 tip and filled with colored royal icing, pipe a series of double loops onto heavy-duty waxed paper (shiny side up). Repeat using the other colors. You will need approximately 6 double loops for each individual cake. Allow to dry overnight.

2 Pipe a small dome of stiff white royal icing on top of each individual iced cake. Carefully peel the iced ribbon loops off the waxed paper and fix in position. Work on one cake at a time and ensure all the loops are facing towards the middle.

To assemble Arrange the finished cakes on an iced stand made with square boards edged in ⅝-inch width ribbon and 3-inch high polystyrene columns (see page 32).

candy stripes

you will need

8-inch round cake covered with marzipan and fondant and placed centrally on an 11-inch board covered with fondant

white royal icing and 3 bright food colors

pastry bags fitted with no. 3 tips

scribe

8-inch round board

⅝-inch width ribbon for the board

fresh flowers to dress

This candy-stripe cake design, hand piped with vertical pinstripes in three bright colors, is eye-catching and fun. Changing the colors to complement the theme or flowers of an occasion is an effective way to completely transform the design. It can be adapted to create a feminine birthday cake, or made bold and bright for a more funky look. I have also used this technique for christening cakes in shades of blue and pink.

1 Divide 1 recipe of fresh royal icing into 3 clean bowls and color each portion to the desired intensity. Spoon the icing into 3 separate pastry bags, each fitted with a no. 3 tip.

2 Using a scribe, mark around an 8-inch board positioned carefully on top of an iced 8-inch cake, to act as the top guide. Pipe one icing color in a vertical line from the top guide to the cake board. Pipe the second color parallel to the first and the third color parallel to the second. Repeat all the way around the cake.

3 Fix ribbon around the edge of the baseboard and dress the top of the finished cake with fresh flowers or a simple piped message, if desired.

3-tier funky candy stripe

As a tiered cake this candy stripe design is particularly dazzling. Here I have combined purple, ruby and yellow candy stripes with fresh tulips, anemones and roses.

catlia lace

you will need

3-tier round cake—4-, 6- and 8-inch tiers covered with marzipan and white fondant, stacked centrally on an 11-inch round board covered with white fondant

12 oz. white fondant to make the ribbon bands

confectioners' sugar

rolling pin

sharp knife

ruler

pastry brush

template (see page 154)

waxed paper

pen

scribe

pastry bags

no. 1.5 and no. 3 tip

white royal icing

paintbrush

topaz luster mixed with alcohol dipping solution

⅝-inch width white ribbon to edge the baseboard

The inspiration for this cake comes from an exquisite piece of lace ribbon. I have adapted the design to work around an iced ribbon band on this small, three-tier stacked cake. The finished cake is presented on a polystyrene block studded with fresh roses to create additional height and drama.

Tip When using a template with a repeating pattern to mark up several tiers, work from the bottom tier upwards. This way you can use just one template, cutting it shorter for the upper tiers. Make sure the join of the design is always at the back of the cake. When decorating a tiered cake, always begin with the top tier and work downwards so the icing is not smudged or damaged.

1 Knead the white fondant until smooth and pliable. Divide into 3 portions (adjusting for the different sizes of tiers). Lightly dust a work surface with confectioners' sugar and roll out a ribbon of icing sufficient to fit all the way around the top tier. Cut the iced ribbon using a knife and ruler to create straight edges top and bottom. Moisten the base of the tier with water and fix the iced ribbon band in position as shown. Repeat with other tiers making sure all the iced ribbon bands join at the back of the cake. Allow to set overnight.

2 Using the template on page 154, trace enough of the lace design onto waxed paper to fit around the bottom tier. With the template in position, use a scribe to prick the design onto the fondant ribbon. Repeat with the middle and top tiers.

3 Fill a pastry bag with a no. 1.5 tip and white royal icing. Pipe the scallops around the top edge of the ribbon, then the central strand of pearls with tiny leaves on each side as shown. Finish with a pearl at the top of each scallop.

4 Fill a pastry bag with a no. 3 tip and white royal icing. Pipe large pearls around the base of each tier. When the icing is dry, brush the scallops and pearl strand and leaves with topaz luster mixed with alcohol dipping solution. Fix ribbon around the baseboard, securing it with a dab of royal icing at the back.

preparing flowers for blocking

you will need

florist's scissors

fresh roses

florist's wires cut to 4-inch lengths

3½-inch deep round polystyrene base
(allows 2 rows of roses)

I like to dress cakes with fresh flowers. There are many varieties and colors available so it is worth experimenting, but I have found roses to be particularly effective for blocking between tiers of a cake or for studding a polystyrene base for display, as here.

1 Trim each rose to leave approximately ¾ inch of stalk. Gently tease a wire into the stalk.

2 Insert the wire into the polystyrene block. Repeat, working around the cake base or tier and ensure the roses are lined up and equal.

The following table is provided as a guide only. The numbers will vary depending on the species of rose, how full blown the flowers are and how tightly you position them next to one another. You may like to include other flowers or greenery to fill any gaps and reduce the cost.

Size of tier	Number of roses required	
	Single row	Double row
6-inch	8	14
8-inch	12	22
10-inch	16	30
12-inch	20	38
14-inch	26	50
16-inch	32	60

Tip For a single row of roses and flowers allow 2 inches between the tiers; for a double row allow 3½ inches and position the upper row in between the flowers on the bottom row. Don't underestimate the number of flowers you will need!

lace brush embroidery

you will need

3-tier cake covered with marzipan and fondant and stacked centrally on a baseboard 3 inches larger than bottom tier, covered with fondant

pastry bags

no. 2 tip

royal icing

1-inch width ribbon to fix around each tier

template (see page 149), optional

paintbrush

topaz luster mixed with dipping alcohol solution

⅝-inch width ribbon to edge baseboard

glue stick (to fix ribbon around baseboard)

fresh rose petals to dress (optional)

A cake covered in delicate hand-iced lace is extremely romantic. I love this design, which was inspired by the handmade lace featured on my own wedding dress. It is essentially made up of three patterns – a large flower, which is brush embroidered, smaller flowers and clusters of berries with leaves – which are repeated randomly over the cake ensuring all the space is filled. It is a good idea to practice piping a section of the lace design onto a spare cake board to get a feel for the pattern before you begin piping it freehand onto the cake.

Tip Fix the ribbon around each tier first and pipe the design on each tier up to the edge of the ribbon. This allows the ribbon to settle flush against the smooth icing on the covered cake.

1 Fill a pastry bag with a no. 2 tip and royal icing. Fix ribbon around the base of each tier. Starting on the top tier hand pipe a small section of the lace design. Pipe the design freehand or use the template on page 149 if you wish.

2 Each time you have piped a large flower, stop and, using a clean, damp paintbrush, gently brush the inner edge only of the piped line towards the centre. Work in small sections over each tier, moving downwards and filling in all the spaces until the whole cake is covered.

3 Once the icing is dry, the whole design can be brushed with a glaze – use topaz luster mixed with alcohol dipping solution. Fix ribbon around the baseboard. If desired, dress the cake with fresh rose petals.

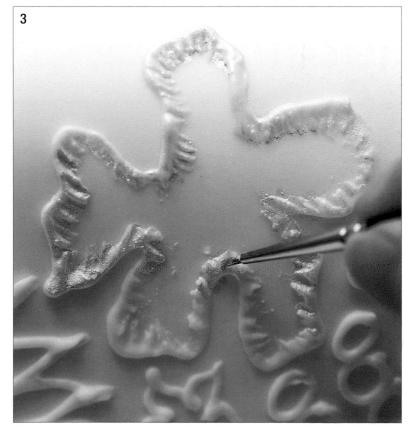

hand-painted orchid

you will need

4-tier round cake—4-, 6-, 8- and 10-inch tiers covered with marzipan and ivory fondant and stacked centrally

13-inch and 16-inch round baseboards covered with ivory fondant

templates (see page 147)

tracing paper

pen

scribe

⅓ oz. cocoa butter

edible color dusts

paintbrush

13-ft. length of ⅜-inch width purple ribbon

royal icing (to fix ribbon around tiers)

10-ft. length of ⅝-inch width purple ribbon

glue stick (to fix ribbon around baseboard)

fresh flowers to dress

Painting onto a cake indulges two of my passions in one! I find it very satisfying both to paint and to create a truly individual decorated cake. I took the inspiration for this orchid cake from a wall-hanging that I have at home. The design is traced and etched onto the cake with layers of edible color dusts suspended in cocoa butter – a bit like painting in oils. Change the flowers, positions or colors to design your own cake.

Tip If you make a mistake while painting, simply absorb the cocoa butter and color with a clean piece of paper towel.

1 Cover the cakes 2 days before decorating and stack the tiers the day before. Trace the orchid and butterfly designs separately onto tracing paper using a pen. Cut each design out and decide where you would like each one to be positioned on the cake, working upwards with the largest flower on the bottom tier. Carefully hold the tracing paper against the cake and use a scribe to mark the design onto the cake. (By gently dragging the scribe over the design it will form an indentation that will be visible when you remove the paper.) Repeat with all the flowers and butterflies. Use a scribe to join the flowers up with a central stalk.

2 Melt the cocoa butter in a saucer suspended over a heat-resistant bowl of boiling water. Tip various edible color dusts onto the edge of the saucer. Use a paintbrush to gently mix the cocoa butter with the color dusts and paint onto the cake. (The more cocoa butter you use, the more translucent the paint colors will be.) Build up colors and layers gradually, allowing time for each to set as the cocoa butter cools. If the cocoa butter starts to cool and harden on the saucer, replace the boiling water in the bowl underneath.

To assemble Once the design is finished and dry, fix the narrower ribbon around each tier, securing it in position at the back of each cake with a dab of royal icing. Glue the wider ribbon around the baseboards. Dress the cake with fresh flowers, such as Vanda orchids.

ballerina fairy

you will need

8-inch petal-shaped cake covered with marzipan and fondant

11-inch petal-shaped board covered with fondant

½-inch width ribbon for the cake

6 medium stamped-out flowers

⅝-inch width ribbon for the board

glue stick (for fixing ribbon around board)

templates (see page 149)

tracing paper

pen

scribe

⅓ oz. cocoa butter

edible color dusts

paintbrush

pastry bag

no. 1.5 tip

2 oz. white royal icing

topaz luster

edible hologram glitter

alcohol dipping solution

Using brush embroidery over a hand-painted design is a versatile way to build up depth. I have two goddaughters and three nieces who particularly approve of this design, which features a sophisticated fairy ballerina together with her fairy dust and army of bumble bees.

1 Position the cake centrally on the covered board. Fix the narrower ribbon around the cake, securing it with royal icing at the back and in each of the indentations of the petal shape. Position a stamped-out flower in each of the indentations of the petal over the ribbon as shown. Fix the wider ribbon around the baseboard. Trace the fairy ballerina and bumble bee designs onto tracing paper. Gently hold the design against the cake and use a scribe to mark the design onto the cake.

2 Melt the cocoa butter in a saucer suspended over a heat-resistant bowl of boiling water. Tip color dusts onto the edge of the saucer. Use a paintbrush to gently mix the cocoa butter with the color dusts as desired and paint onto the cake. Build up colors and layers, allowing time for each to set as the cocoa butter cools. If the cocoa butter starts to cool and harden on the saucer, replace the boiling water in the bowl underneath.

3 Fill a pastry bag with a no. 1.5 tip and fresh white royal icing. Pipe around the outline of the fairy's skirt and the wings of the bumble bees. Use a damp paintbrush to gently brush the icing line inwards to create a brush embroidery effect. Pipe tiny pearls at the fairy's fingers to resemble fairy dust. Allow to dry. Mix a little topaz luster with edible hologram glitter and enough alcohol dipping solution to create a thin paste. Brush over the royal icing with a paintbrush.

birds of paradise

you will need

2-tier hexagonal cake covered with marzipan and caramel-ivory colored fondant

baseboard 3 inches larger than the bottom tier, covered with fondant

½-inch width ribbon to fix around cake tiers and edge the baseboard

royal icing (for fixing ribbon around cake tiers and baseboard)

templates (see page 148)

tracing paper

pen

scribe

⅓ oz. cocoa butter

edible color dusts

paintbrush

fresh flowers to dress

I was inspired by the beautiful detail on a silk brisé fan for this design, which is full of Eastern promise and romance, befitting a special wedding or anniversary cake. I have chosen to paint with earth and spice tones of saffron, basil, ocher and burnt sienna and to dress the cake with fresh golden-shower orchids and gloriosa lilies.

1 Stack the cakes and position on the baseboard, following the instructions on page 35. Fix the ribbon around the base of each tier and around the baseboard, securing with royal icing at the back. Trace the birds of paradise designs (see page 148) separately onto tracing paper using a pen. Gently hold the template against the cake and use a scribe to mark the design onto the cake.

2 Melt the cocoa butter in a saucer suspended over a heat-resistant bowl of boiling water. Tip color dusts onto the edge of the saucer. Use a paintbrush to gently mix the cocoa butter with the color dusts as desired and paint onto the cake. Build up colors and layers gradually, allowing time for each to set as the cocoa butter cools. Finally, dress the cake with fresh flowers.

Tip If the cocoa butter starts to cool and harden on the saucer, replace the boiling water in the bowl underneath.

woven ribbon

you will need

8-inch round cake covered with marzipan and hot-pink fondant, placed on an 11-inch round board covered with fondant

glue stick

5-ft. length of ⅝-inch width citrus-green ribbon

royal icing

pastry bag

10-ft. length of ⅛-inch width citrus-green ribbon

ruler

white paper

pen

sharp scissors

scribe

ribbon-insertion tool

fresh flowers to dress

The first time I saw ribbon inserted into a cake I was convinced that the ribbon had literally been threaded through the icing. In fact, this is an illusion: little snippets of ribbon are actually tucked into pre-marked slits. It's an extremely effective and relatively simple way to decorate a cake. This triple-looped design works well on a round cake and looks very striking as a tiered wedding cake. The ribbon loops are topped with handmade ribbon bows in the same color. I have used numerous colors of ribbon on many different colored cakes – but this is definitely the first time for hot pink and citrus green!

Tip If you're using this design on a multitiered cake, make sure that you keep the base point of the loops the same on each cake (you can adjust the top height of the loops if necessary).

1 Allow the covered cake to dry overnight before decorating it. Glue ⅝-inch width ribbon around the edge of the baseboard. Fix ⅝-inch width ribbon around the base of the cake, securing the join at the back with royal icing. Measure the circumference of the cake by wrapping ⅛-inch width ribbon around the cake, then holding the length of ribbon against a ruler. Divide this length by 3 to give you the distance between each ribbon loop.

2 Hold a ruler against the cake and measure from the base of the cake to the height you want the top of the ribbon loops to be (ideally they should be approximately ½ inch from the top of the cake). Similarly, measure the lowest point of the loop (about ¾ inch from the base, depending on the overall height of the cake).

3 Measuring from the corner of a clean piece of paper, mark the height of the top of the ribbon loop along one edge. Fold over the edge of the paper at this point to form a strip. Carefully cut the strip from the rest of the sheet of paper, then mark the distance between the ribbon loops on the long edge of the paper strip. Cut off the remainder of the strip. Fold the strip of paper in half crosswise.

4 Mark the lowest point of the ribbon loop on the folded edge of the paper strip, then draw half a loop/arc freehand reaching from the lowest point at the fold up to the top of the opposite outside edge.

5 Cut along the line of the loop/arc. Open out the paper to show a perfectly symmetrical loop.

6 Hold the template against the cake and use a scribe to trace the loop onto the cake, starting at the top of the loop. Repeat twice more and the loops should join up at the back of the cake.

7 Working from left to right, use the ribbon-insertion tool to follow the line of the loops, firmly pressing it into the cake until the base touches the scribed line. Insert the left-hand prong into the last slit made. This will ensure the slits are evenly spaced. Continue all around the cake.

8 Cut some 1-inch lengths from ⅛-inch width ribbon. Starting at the top of a loop, use the ribbon-insertion tool to tuck the left-hand side of the ribbon in first. Fold ribbon over the second slit and push in snugly. Repeat around the cake.

To assemble Make 3 simple ribbon bows from the remainder of the ribbon and fix them into position at the top of the loops with royal icing. Finally, dress the top of the cake with fresh flowers.

chocolate cakes

chocolate

Chocolate cakes are visually stunning and decadent. They are also generally sculptured and therefore less precise than iced cakes. This can be very appealing to less experienced – and more expressive – cake decorators, as most of these cakes are created without pastry bags and tips.

tempering chocolate

I like to cover individual cakes with pure melted chocolate. The taste and finish is a clean, crisp chocolate with all the appeal of a decadent chocolate truffle. However, in order to work effectively with melted chocolate it must first be tempered (or precrystallized) to achieve the shine, correct melting properties and stability of quality chocolate. Most importantly, tempering chocolate will prevent blooming (unsightly white streaks in the chocolate as it resets).

3

1 Break the chocolate into small pieces and place in a large clean bowl over a pan of simmering water. (Do not boil – if water or steam comes into contact with the chocolate, it will turn into a solid block. Water and chocolate do not mix!) Stir the chocolate while melting to ensure even heating but try to avoid creating air bubbles. Heat chocolate to 113°F.

2 Replace the hot water with cold water and stir continuously until the chocolate cools to 81°F. Occasionally it may be necessary to add additional cool water underneath the bowl.

3 Now replace the cold water with warm water and raise the temperature of the chocolate to 89–90°F for dark chocolate, 86–89°F for milk chocolate and 82–84°F for white chocolate. Maintain the appropriate temperature while dipping. If chocolate cools or warms outside of these temperatures, you will need to temper it again.

4 Test the temper of the chocolate before starting to dip. This can be done by spreading a small amount onto aluminium foil and allowing it to cool. It should be smooth and shiny with no dull or wet areas. Streaks may indicate poor temper or a lack of mixing. If the results are unsatisfactory, you will need to retemper the chocolate before proceeding.

Tip The room used for tempering and dipping chocolate should be 68°F and draft free. If the room or chocolate is too warm, the chocolates may have large "tailings" or feet. If the chocolate becomes too warm or too cool it will lack shine or show signs of bloom. Low humidity, no strong odors and good air circulation are also recommended. Having a good thermometer with a range from 60 to 122°F is advisable.

poured chocolate ganache icing

For a decadent covering for the chocolate truffle or luscious lemon cakes, pour smooth chocolate ganache icing over a cake that has been sandwiched, surrounded and topped with buttercream. This recipe differs slightly from the chocolate ganache I blend with buttercream for the filling in that I have added butter, which allows the ganache icing to pour smoothly and remain glossy.

1

dark chocolate ganache icing

you will need

18 oz. semisweet chocolate (70% cocoa solids), broken into pieces

9 oz. unsalted butter, cut into small pieces

9 tbsp. heavy cream

yields about 3 cups

1 Place the chocolate and butter in a bowl. In a pan, bring cream to the boil and pour over chocolate and butter. Stir with a wooden spoon until chocolate and butter have melted and icing is smooth.

2 While it is still warm, pour the ganache liberally over a prepared cake standing on a wire rack set on a piece of waxed paper. Use a metal spatula or the back of a metal spoon to move the chocolate over the cake top and sides. Holding the rack with both hands, gently tap it to allow the ganache icing to even itself and settle over the cake.

To store Spoon any excess ganache into a container and store in the refrigerator for up to 2 weeks. Ganache is suitable for freezing for up to 1 month: allow it to thaw overnight at room temperature, then gently heat in a microwave or in a bowl over simmering water.

2

size of cake	6-inch	8-inch	10-inch	12-inch
quantity of ganache to cover	½ recipe	1 recipe	1½ recipes	2 recipes

white chocolate ganache icing

Heat the cream until it has just boiled to avoid a skim on the top of the cream. (If you overboil it, pour it over the chocolate through a strainer.) Pour over white chocolate and stir until smooth. Adding melted butter will create a higher gloss to the icing, but is not essential.

you will need

1 cup + 2 tbsp. heavy cream

18 oz. white chocolate, chips or chopped

1–2 tbsp. unsalted butter, melted (optional)

yields about 2¾ cups

chocolate plastic

Chocolate plastic is a combination of pure chocolate with a sugar stock syrup – effectively glucose – which makes chocolate malleable, enabling you to roll it out to cover a cake or hand mold it to create the fans, roses and leaves used in many of the designs shown here. Chocolate plastic has all the taste of chocolate, but with the texture of fondant and gives a smooth, firm finish to a cake. You can use chocolate plastic to cover a cake in exactly the same way as you would marzipan and fondant: follow the quantities given for marzipan for a single layer and for fondant for a second layer (see pages 25 and 27). To make milk chocolate plastic, knead together dark and white chocolate plastic.

stock syrup

you will need

1 cup + 2 tbsp. water

⅝ cup superfine sugar

6 tbsp. light corn syrup

yields 2 cups

Place all the ingredients into a saucepan and bring to the boil. Remove from the heat and leave to cool. This recipe will provide slightly more than necessary to create the white chocolate plastic recipe below.

white chocolate plastic

you will need

3 lb. 14 oz. white chocolate, broken into pieces

14 oz. cocoa butter

1¾ cups light corn syrup

1¼ cups stock syrup

yields 5½ lb.

1 Melt the chocolate in a microwave or place it in a clean, heat-resistant bowl over a saucepan of simmering water. Melt the cocoa butter in a microwave or place it in a clean, heat-resistant bowl over a saucepan of simmering water. (It is important to melt the cocoa butter and chocolate separately as they melt at different rates and both need to be melted for the recipe to work.) Mix the chocolate and cocoa butter together and stir well. Measure the corn syrup and stock syrup together and warm slightly in the microwave. (This allows all the ingredients to be at a similar temperature for the final mix.)

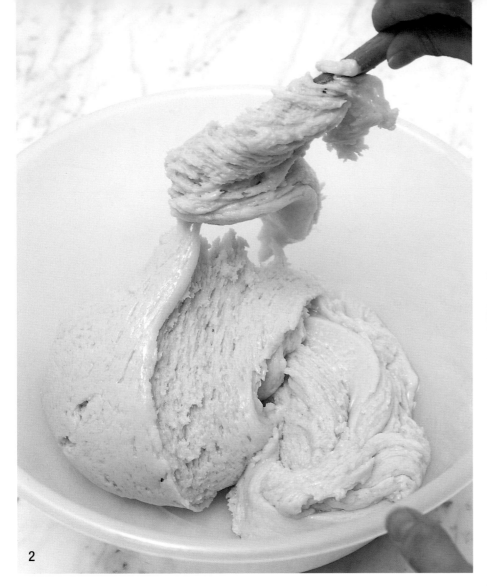

2

Tip If the paste is very stiff, place in a microwave for 10 seconds on medium heat to soften. If it is too soft or warm, refrigerate it for a couple of minutes to harden slightly.

2 Pour chocolate over corn and stock syrups and mix well with a wooden spoon until smooth. Transfer the mixture into a clean large freezer bag and leave overnight at room temperature to set.

3 When ready to use, knead the chocolate plastic until smooth and pliable. Roll out on a surface lightly dusted with confectioners' sugar.

3

dark chocolate plastic

Melt the chocolate in a microwave or place it in a clean, heat-resistant bowl over a saucepan of simmering water. Heat to 110°F. Heat the glucose syrup separately to the same temperature. Pour the syrup into the melted chocolate and stir with a wooden spoon until thoroughly combined. Allow to cool completely. Transfer the mixture into a clean large freezer bag and leave overnight at room temperature to set. To use, peel away the bag and knead the chocolate until smooth and pliable.

you will need

2 lb. 12 oz. dark chocolate, 55% maximum cocoa solids, broken into pieces

2 lb. 4 oz. glucose syrup

yields 5 lb.

piping chocolate

Piping with chocolate is similar to piping with royal icing. You can use either pure, melted, tempered chocolate or a cooled, poured chocolate ganache.

piping melted chocolate

For pure melted chocolate it is not advisable to use a tip, as the chocolate tends to set as it comes into contact with the stainless steel of the tip, causing it to clog up. Simply fill a pastry bag with melted chocolate and snip the end. Use this technique to pipe messages onto cakes or to create chocolate decorations. To make the ones shown opposite, pipe a central loop onto waxed paper (shiny side up). Still holding the bag, pipe a second loop lower and outside of the first. Repeat with 2 more loops – always coming back to the base center. Allow the decorations to cool before carefully peeling them off the waxed paper.

piping chocolate ganache

The cooled ganache used for pouring over a cake (see page 67) also works very well for piping. It flows well through a pastry bag filled with a tip. Fill a bag with a plain no. 4 tip to create large pearls around the base of a cake. Use various tips to create scrolls, stars and flowers and other decorations as shown. If the ganache becomes too stiff to pipe, gently heat it in a microwave or in a bowl over simmering water for a few moments before continuing.

chocolate glazing lusters

Chocolate can be dusted with glazing luster to add color to the finished cake. Lusters are available in many colors including copper, bronze, sapphire, ruby, jade, gold and topaz. Use a paintbrush to brush the powder lusters onto hand-molded chocolate-plastic roses, leaves and fans to develop the color.

adding luster to a chocolate cake

Lusters can be added to whole cakes, such as this dark chocolate-plastic helter-skelter, to provide a metallic sheen. Dark chocolate picks up the strong luster colors particularly well. As with small chocolate decorations, simply brush the powders on with a large paintbrush while the chocolate is still fresh. You can also add lusters to a cake freshly covered in a poured dark chocolate ganache. Gently flick a paintbrush of luster across one corner of the top of the cake before dressing it with hand-molded chocolate roses and leaves and/or fresh fruit.

chocolate ganache torte

you will need

8-inch chocolate truffle torte, layered with chocolate ganache buttercream and fresh raspberries, placed on an 8-inch board

wire rack

waxed paper

ladle

1 recipe poured chocolate ganache (see page 67)

metal spatula

pastry bag

no. 4 tip

fresh berries and hand-molded chocolate roses (see page 75) to decorate

The chocolate truffle torte here is layered with chocolate ganache buttercream and fresh raspberries with lashings of poured chocolate ganache. To finish I have dressed the cake with fresh berries and hand-molded chocolate roses.

1 Place the prepared cake on a wire rack over a sheet of waxed paper. Liberally pour ladlefuls of the chocolate ganache over the cake. Make gentle circular swirls with the bottom of the ladle over the ganache to encourage it to run down and coat the sides of the cake.

2 Gently hold the sides of the wire rack, lift it up and tap it down gently but firmly to level the ganache and remove any air bubbles. Use a metal spatula to ensure the top and sides are evenly coated and textured.

3 Lift the cake off the wire rack using a metal spatula and set on a serving plate. Fill a pastry bag with a large plain tip and 2 large spoonfuls of the chocolate ganache. Pipe beads of chocolate around the base of the cake to neaten the edges. Dress the top of the cake with fresh berries and hand-molded chocolate roses.

Tip For a wedding cake, pour the ganache over the cake but rather than using a spatula, allow the ganache to find its own level to create a smooth finish. You may like to first cover the tiers with an initial coat of white chocolate plastic for a professional touch.

chocolate roses

you will need

3 (2-inch) round individual cakes

3½ oz. each of white, dark and milk chocolate plastic

plastic sheeting

metal spatula

3 (8-inch) lengths of ⅝-inch width cream, gold and dark brown grosgrain ribbon

1 oz. white chocolate, melted

1 oz. dark chocolate, melted

pastry bags

Individual chocolate-covered cakes look stunning dressed with these hand-molded chocolate roses. They are perfect for an elegant wedding, served for dessert dressed on a plate with a little raspberry coulis or coconut ice cream. The quantity of chocolate plastic given here will make approximately 8–10 roses of 2-inch diameter or cover three mini cakes and make a rose for the top of each as shown opposite. The roses will store well for up to six months in a cool, dry container.

1 Warm a small amount of chocolate plastic between your palms and roll into a ball. Place between 2 sheets of plastic. Flatten quickly with the base of your palm, then, using your index finger, flatten two-thirds of the way round the ball, leaving a thicker base.

2 Remove the chocolate from the plastic sheeting and, holding the thicker base, gently roll the chocolate to form the center of the rose.

3 Repeat step 1 to create 4 more petals. Wrap a petal around the rose center, then fix the final 3 petals so they overlap one another. Gently tease the petals into shape. Slice the base off the finished rose using a metal spatula.

To assemble Cover each cake with a double layer of white, milk or dark chocolate plastic. Attach ribbon around the base of each cake, securing with melted chocolate. Pipe a small amount of melted chocolate onto the base of the chocolate roses and fix into position on the cakes.

Tip This method for hand-molding chocolate roses can also be used for making roses from fondant.

individual chocolate rose stand

Set a number of individual chocolate-rose-decorated cakes on a stand for a special occasion. Here I have added a 6-inch top tier for the cutting ceremony. These cakes are shelf stable and will not spoil if left out of the refrigerator throughout a reception.

tricolored fans and roses

you will need

3-tier cake—4-, 7- and 10-inch cakes
covered with white, milk and dark
chocolate plastic respectively, placed on
boards the same size, stacked centrally

13-inch baseboard covered with
dark chocolate plastic

white, milk and dark chocolate to fix
the roses and fans into position

2 lb. white chocolate plastic

3 lb. dark chocolate plastic

confectioners' sugar

rolling pin

12 white, 16 milk and 20 dark chocolate
roses (see page 75)

⅝-inch width brown grosgrain ribbon

This chocolate creation is an adaptation of the wedding cake I designed and created for Sir Paul McCartney and Heather Mills. Each tier of the cake is covered in chocolate then adorned with hand-molded roses and fans. The effect is an amazing sculpture of chocolate that needs no further decoration of fruit or flowers.

1 Melt the chocolates separately. Knead the chocolate plastic until smooth and pliable. Use 13 oz. each of white and dark plastic to make milk chocolate plastic. Lightly dust a work surface with confectioners' sugar and roll each of the 3 types of plastic to a large square ¼ inch thick. Cut out rectangles of varying sizes. Take a rectangle of plastic and pleat it. Pinch the center and fold in half to make a fan.

2 Beginning with the bottom tier, fix the dark chocolate roses and fans in position with melted dark chocolate. Allow the fans and roses to protrude over the top edge of the cake tier but do not curl them inwards.

3 Repeat with the milk chocolate middle tier and finish with the white chocolate fans and roses on the top tier. As long as there is no fresh fruit inside the cake it can remain in this state stored in a cool dry place (but not refrigerated) for up to 3 days. Edge the board with ribbon once the cake is decorated.

white velvet rose

you will need

3-tier cake—4-, 7- and 10-inch tiers, covered with white chocolate plastic and placed on boards the same size

13-inch and 16-inch boards covered with white chocolate plastic

3½ oz. white chocolate, melted

pastry bag

250 (approx) white chocolate scrolls

40 hand-molded white chocolate fans (see page 76)

30 hand-molded white chocolate roses (see page 75)

⅜-inch width cream grosgrain ribbon to edge baseboards

fresh rose petals to dress (optional)

Chocolate scrolls or cigarillos will transform a simple chocolate cake into a truly spectacular one. They are commercially available in white and dark chocolate and handle extremely well. The cake should be initially prepared with buttercream and covered with a layer of ganache (single tier) or chocolate plastic (multiple tiers).

size of square tier	number of scrolls (approx.)
4 inches	50
6 inches	75
8 inches	100
10 inches	120
12 inches	150
14 inches	170
16 inches	200

Tip The hand-molded roses can be made well in advance, but make the fans as you go, using them to fill any gaps.

1 Place the bottom tier onto the double baseboards, fixing into position with melted chocolate. Fill a pastry bag with melted white chocolate. Snip the end off the bag and, working on a 4-inch section at a time, pipe trails of chocolate onto the sides of the cake. Stick the chocolate scrolls onto the cake evenly with joins against the cake. Repeat until all cake tiers are surrounded and leave until the chocolate has set firm.

2 When you are ready to dress the cake, stack the tiers as shown on page 35, fixing them into position with a little melted white chocolate. Working on one tier at a time, position the white chocolate fans and roses around the tiers, finishing with a flourish on the top tier. Attach ribbon around the baseboards, securing it with melted chocolate at the back of the cake. Dress the base of the cake with fresh rose petals, if desired.

chocolate scroll birthday

For a truly decadent birthday cake, decorate a chocolate truffle torte with dark chocolate scrolls. Position a fondant plaque in the center of the cake and decorate with fresh seasonal berries.

individual ganache bites

These individual bite-size cakes are covered with an initial coat of white chocolate plastic then enrobed with tempered chocolate. Each is topped with a chocolate-dipped strawberry and displayed on a white chocolate stand. This cake is very popular for cocktail parties, for which the little cakes are an ideal size. Be sure to make enough! I use a half-depth cake to make these bites. This keeps the height down so they are easier to eat with your fingers.

you will need

8-inch single-layer square chocolate truffle torte, split in half horizontally and sandwiched with chocolate ganache buttercream (yields 25 bites)

8-inch square luscious lemon cake split in half horizontally, one half split again and sandwiched with lemon curd buttercream (yields 25 bites)

1½- and 2-inch round cutters

pastry brush

10½ oz. apricot jam

rolling pin

3 lb. 8 oz. white chocolate plastic

wire rack

waxed paper

2 lb. 4 oz. white chocolate

small ladle or spoon

pastry bag

2 lb. 4 oz. dark chocolate

50 small strawberries

3-tier white chocolate stand

1 Cut rounds of cake using the 1½-inch cutter and brush each small cake with apricot jam.

2 Cover each cake with a single layer of white chocolate plastic. (Use the larger cutter to trim excess.) Keep the chocolate and lemon cakes separate. Working in small batches of 5–8 at a time, place the prepared chocolate cakes on a wire rack over a sheet of waxed paper.

3 Temper white chocolate and pour spoonfuls over the lemon cakes. Excess chocolate can be reused. Fill a pastry bag with white chocolate and snip the end. Drizzle white chocolate over the cakes in a crisscross design. Temper the dark chocolate and repeat the above to cover and decorate chocolate cakes.

To assemble Dip strawberries in tempered chocolate and allow to set on waxed paper. Present the bites on a chocolate stand with a chocolate-dipped strawberry placed on each.

cakes for events

valentine heart

you will need

10-inch heart-shaped cake covered with dark chocolate (poured ganache or chocolate plastic), placed on a board the same shape and size or on a plate

3½ oz. dark chocolate (if cake is covered with chocolate plastic)

pastry bag

120 (approx) dark chocolate scrolls

2¼ lb. strawberries

10 (approx) dark chocolate decorative pieces (see page 70)

5-ft. length of red organza ribbon

Oh, the romance, the seduction, the decadence! I have used a heart-shaped pan to bake this chocolate truffle torte and layered the tiers with chocolate ganache buttercream and fresh sliced strawberries. The cake is surrounded with dark chocolate scrolls and the top packed with fresh strawberries and hand-piped chocolate decorations. Serve it, ideally for breakfast, with a glass of chilled pink champagne – your Valentine will be spellbound!

1 If the cake has been covered in dark chocolate plastic, melt the dark chocolate and pour into a pastry bag. Snip the end off the bag and pipe a trail of dark chocolate over a 4-inch section of the side of the cake. Fix scrolls into position with the join on each scroll touching the cake. Work all the way around the cake.

2 Brush the top of the cake with melted chocolate and gently set the fresh strawberries into position. Use the chocolate decorative pieces to fill any small gaps. To finish, tie the cake with a red organza ribbon and bow.

Tip If you cover the cake with poured ganache you will not need the melted chocolate to stick the scrolls into position – they will adhere to the ganache. Always use chocolate plastic rather than ganache to cover a multitier cake as it is more stable.

rosebud heart

you will need

3-tier heart cake—6-, 9- and 12-inch tiers covered with ivory fondant and stacked centrally

15-inch and 18-inch heart-shaped boards covered with ivory fondant

ivory, pink and lime-green gum paste

small rolling pin

1½-inch rose cutter

ball tool

soft foam pad

paintbrush

sugar glue

1-inch calyx cutter

1-inch width ivory ribbon for the cakes

royal icing

pastry bag

no. 1.5 tip

15 silver balls (¼-inch diameter)

⅜-inch width ivory ribbon to edge baseboards

glue stick

Heart-shaped cakes are very romantic, but they're often considered to be rather old fashioned. For this special cake I have stacked three hearts, surrounded the tiers with a wide satin ribbon and studded the lips of the cake with delicate handmade sugar rosebuds. By adding just a few silver dragées on the sides of the tiers, I have created a clean, modern, stylish cake befitting the most contemporary of occasions.

2 Roll out the green gum paste very thinly. Cut out a calyx shape using a calyx cutter. Use the ball tool and soft pad to gently shape each of the calyx strands. Brush the center of the calyx with sugar glue and set the rosebud on top. Gently press the calyx into position around the rosebud. For this cake you will need 15 pink rosebuds and 15 ivory ones.

1 To make each rosebud, roll a pea-sized ball of pink gum paste into a cone shape and allow to firm for 1 hour. Roll out a small piece of pink gum paste very thinly and cut out a small rose shape using the cutter. Using a ball tool with a foam pad, gently curve each petal of the rose. Brush a small amount of sugar glue in the center and place the cone on top. Gently fold a petal up and around the central cone, pinching together the edges to create a sharp point. Push the opposite petal up around the first, then tuck the remaining petals around to create a delicate rosebud. Repeat with ivory gum paste.

To assemble Fix lengths of 1-inch width ivory ribbon around each tier and secure at the back with royal icing. Place the sugar rosebuds on the lips of the cake and baseboards until you are happy with the layout. Pipe a small ball of royal icing onto the bottom of each one and secure into position. Pipe small balls of icing onto the sides of the cake and top tier only and fix silver balls in place. Finally, edge the baseboard with the narrow ribbon, securing it in place at the back with glue stick.

daisy chain

you will need

4-inch round cake covered with marzipan and white fondant placed on a 6-inch round board covered with white fondant

rolling pin

2 oz. white gum paste

1-inch daisy cutter

sharp blade

ball tool

sponge mat

sugar glue

2 oz. yellow gum paste

paintbrush

scribe

sugar pollen granules mixed with egg-yellow food coloring

pastry bag and no. 2 tip

green royal icing

40-inch length of wide sheer ribbon

He loves me... He loves me not... He loves me... This design is effective and versatile yet so clean and simple. The daisy heads are made from colored sugar, then chained together with piped green royal icing. The cake has been finished with a sheer green ribbon. This is also a great design to use on individual cakes.

1 To make the daisies, roll out the white gum paste very thinly. The paste dries out very quickly so only work a few at a time. You will need 2 cut-outs for each daisy. Cut each petal in half using a sharp blade.

2 Using a small ball tool, and with cut-out daisies on a sponge mat, draw petals towards the center of the daisy. Place a daisy cut-out over another so that the petals overlap. Fix into position with sugar glue.

3 Roll a small piece of yellow gum paste into a dome. Brush with sugar glue, spear on a scribe and dip into yellow pollen granules. Allow to dry.

4 Carefully position the daisy center inside the flower, securing it in place with sugar glue.

To assemble Pipe a green chain onto the top of the cake and, while it is still wet, press each daisy head into position. Tie the sheer ribbon around the bottom of the cake.

easter bunny

you will need

8-inch oval-shaped cake covered with marzipan and mint-green fondant

12-inch oval board covered with mint-green fondant and edged with ⅝-inch width mint-green ribbon

2-inch round individual cakes covered with marzipan and mint-green fondant, edged with ⅝-inch width yellow or orange ribbon

7 oz. white modeling paste

orange, pink and green food coloring

dried spaghetti

wooden pick

white and yellow gum paste

ball tool and soft foam pad

sugar glue

paintbrush

white and black royal icing

pastry bag

small rolling pin

1-inch daffodil cutter

6½-ft. length of colorful wired ribbon

This Easter cake is just gorgeous! I wanted to create an oval cake tied with a big, colorful, wired ribbon to create the essence of a giant Easter egg and offset the cake on a large oval board, which leaves space to dress it with hand-decorated mini cakes. This idea is great for a party and the little cakes can be presented to each guest or taken home in a gift box.

1 Shape the bunny's body and head from white modeling paste as shown. Insert a strand of dried spaghetti to protrude 1 inch from the top of the body and use a wooden pick or the end of a paintbrush to indent the 2 eyes. Make 2 front and 2 back legs and a tail from white gum paste. Make the pieces for the bow tie from orange modeling paste. Prepare a small piece of white modeling paste to resemble the teeth and mark with a wooden pick. Make 2 jowls from white paste, marking on whiskers with a wooden pick, and a small triangular nose from pink paste. Make 2 ears from white and pink modeling paste and use a ball tool over a foam pad to gently press the pastes together and bend the ears. Insert a strand of dried spaghetti into each ear to protrude ¾ inch.

2 Use sugar glue to assemble the elements of the bunny. Attach the legs and tail to the body as shown, then assemble the bow-tie pieces and fix to the front of the body. Attach the teeth to the head, then fix the jowls into position and add the pink nose. Push the ears into position and pipe eyes with white royal icing followed by black royal icing for the pupils. Carefully position the head onto the body of the bunny.

3 To make each carrot, roll a piece of orange modeling paste into a cone and use a wooden pick to mark indentations across it. Roll a small cone of green modeling paste to make the carrot top and mark the flat end with a cross. Indent the flat end of the carrot with a wooden pick and gently push in the green carrot top, securing it with sugar glue.

4 To make each daffodil, roll out a piece of yellow gum paste very thinly and cut out a trumpet and 2 sets of petals using a daffodil cutter. Feather the edges of the trumpet and petals with a ball tool. Brush sugar glue in the center of a petal and place another over the top so petals sit between the ones below. Roll the trumpet into a cylinder and fix into position with sugar glue.

To assemble Place the cake onto the board, offset to one side, and fix it into position with royal icing. Tie wired ribbon around the bottom of the cake and finish with a large double bow. Ice the bunny into position on top of the cake and decorate with sugar daffodils and carrots. Secure a carrot or daffodil on the top of each of the mini cakes and set these around the cake on the board.

summer pavlova

you will need

11 oz. white chocolate

20 small individual meringues and one 8-inch one (see page 20)

2½ cups heavy cream

1¼ cups crème pâtissière (or fresh custard sauce)

6 oz. ripe mango

1 pint of fresh raspberries

1 pint of fresh strawberries

at least 30 edible flowers

3-tier white chocolate stand— 9-, 11- and 13-inch tiers (see page 33)

I designed this cake for a client having an English country wedding in her garden. It was a glorious summer's day. Individual vanilla meringues are pre-lined with white chocolate, filled on site with a mango crème mousseline and topped with fresh seasonal berries and edible flowers. I set them on a white chocolate stand with a larger pavlova on the top for the bride and groom to cut. You may be able to find edible flowers in the herb section of a good supermarket. Alternatively you could ask your local greengrocer to order them especially for you – or even grow your own!

Tip The meringues are filled with fresh cream, which should be kept out of the refrigerator for no longer than 4 hours. Plan your timing carefully as once filled and displayed they should be eaten within 4 hours.

1 Melt the chocolate in a clean bowl in a microwave or over a small saucepan of simmering water. Use a pastry brush to brush the center of each meringue with melted chocolate. Allow to set.

2 In a large clean bowl whip the cream until it forms soft peaks. Stir in the fresh crème pâtissière. Cut the flesh from the mango and blend to make a puree. Stir the mango puree into the cream. Gently crush ½ the raspberries and slice the strawberries and fold into the cream.

3 Place a generous spoonful of the cream carefully on each meringue and fill the large one. Dress with the remainder of the strawberries and finish with an edible flower on each pavlova.

To assemble Carefully set the pavlova on the white chocolate stand, starting with the bottom tier and working upwards. Place the larger pavlova on the top.

winter pavlova

you will need

14 oz. dark chocolate

36 individual hazelnut meringues (see page 20)

3 (14-oz.) cans apricots in syrup

3¾ cups heavy cream

18 cape gooseberries

20 piped chocolate decorations (see page 70)

zest and juice of 3 medium lemons

4-tier dark chocolate stand (see page 33)

This is an adaptation of a delicious hazelnut meringue gâteau my Mother used to make when I was a child. Apricots have an amazing affinity with hazelnut meringue and each is served here with a delicious apricot coulis. To toast the hazelnuts, place them on a baking sheet and bake in the center of the oven for 15–20 minutes or until deep golden brown, then rub off the skins and finely chop the nuts.

1 Melt the chocolate in a clean bowl in a microwave or over a small saucepan of simmering water. Use a pastry brush to brush the center of each meringue with melted chocolate. Allow to set.

2 Drain the apricots, reserving the syrup for the coulis. Blend the apricots to make a puree. In a large clean bowl, whip the cream until it gently forms soft peaks. Carefully fold 6 rounded tablespoons of apricot puree into the cream. Place a generous spoonful of the cream onto each meringue. Dress some with a single cape gooseberry and others with a chocolate decoration.

3 To make the coulis, add reserved apricot syrup to the remaining apricot puree. Add lemon zest and juice to the sauce, stir well and chill. Serve with the meringues.

To assemble Carefully set the filled meringues on the dark chocolate - covered stand, starting with the bottom tier and working upwards one tier at a time.

chocolate bonfire

you will need

10-inch single-layer square chocolate truffle torte layered with chocolate ganache buttercream

2-, 3-, 4- and 5-inch cutters

6-inch round board

1 recipe of chocolate ganache buttercream

18 oz. dark chocolate plastic

rolling pin

confectioners' sugar

sharp knife

ruby, gold, sapphire and copper lusters

edible varnish (optional)

18 oz. fresh autumnal berries and fruit (raspberries, grapes, blackberries, blueberries, cape gooseberries, cherries)

indoor sparklers to decorate (optional)

Ideal Halloween food – rich layers of chocolate torte with lashings of chocolate ganache buttercream, wrapped up in dark chocolate and set alight with fireworks. I have lustered the chocolate with fiery colors and dressed the cake with autumnal berries. This cake is a smaller version of the white helter-skelter with strawberries (see page 137) and as such is constructed entirely from cake without the need for a polystyrene cone.

1 Using the 4 different sizes of cutter, cut out 4 rounds of cake from the single-tier chocolate torte. Place the largest round on the 6-inch round board. Use buttercream to stack the cakes together and cover the sides.

2 Knead the dark chocolate plastic until smooth and pliable. Divide into two and roll one half on a work surface lightly dusted with confectioners' sugar into a long strip approximately 18 x 4 inches. Use a sharp knife to neaten both long edges, then, with the end of a rolling pin, feather one of the long edges (see page 137). Beginning at the bottom of the cake and with the straight edge of the chocolate plastic strip flush with the bottom of the cake, carefully wrap the chocolate around the cake as shown.

3 Repeat with the next piece of chocolate plastic, creating interesting pockets and shapes as you work upwards, finishing with a flourish. Gild the chocolate with strong fiery lusters and spray with edible varnish if desired. Just before serving, dress the cake with fresh berries, placing them in the pockets created by the chocolate plastic covering. Push indoor sparklers into the cake, if desired.

halloween cookies

The ideal trick or treat gift – handmade spiced cookies in the shape of bats and pumpkins are decorated with fondant and colored royal icing. These cookies are fun to make with children, who can create the scariest or happiest pumpkin faces.

amaryllis christmas

you will need

8-inch round cake covered with marzipan and white fondant

11-inch round board covered with white fondant

7 oz. white gum paste

old-gold edible food coloring

small rolling pin

paintbrush

gold luster

4-inch holly cutter

marking tool or wooden pick

sponge

5½-ft. length of ⅜-inch width gold ribbon (for ribbon loops)

11-ft. length of ⅜-inch width white ribbon (for ribbon loops)

26-gauge white and green florist's wires, cut into 4-inch lengths

white and green florist's tape

21 large white stamens

small veining rolling pin

3-inch amaryllis cutter

4-inch amaryllis veining mold

ball tool and soft foam pad

green dusting powder

pastry bag filled with white royal icing

2½-ft. length of 1-inch width white ribbon and 2½-ft. length of ⅜-inch width gold ribbon (for the cake)

glue stick

3-ft. length of ⅜-inch width white ribbon (for the board)

½-inch diameter posy pick

White amaryllis are one of my favorite flowers and, as they are available in the winter, are a natural choice for this luxurious gold and white Christmas cake. This would make a perfect design for a special wedding anniversary celebrated at this time of year: simply change the color of the ribbon – gold for 50 years, ruby for 40 years or silver for 25 years.

1 Knead gum paste until soft and pliable. Reserve half for the amaryllis petals and color half the remainder old gold. Roll out thinly using a small rolling pin. Use a paintbrush to cover with gold luster. Cut out 4 holly leaves and score veins with a marking tool. Arrange leaves on the cake. Make 4 white leaves with white gum paste and position them between the gold ones. Use pieces of sponge to hold leaves in place and leave to dry.

2 Cut gold ribbon into 3 lengths of 6 inches and 3 lengths of 12 inches. Cut white ribbon into 6 lengths of 6 inches and 6 of 12 inches. Fold one end of a long length of ribbon over to create a loop with a tail approximately 4 inches long. Hold one of the short lengths against the other side of the loop.

3 Hold the ends of the loops against a white florist's wire. Secure in place with white florist's tape, winding it all the way to the bottom of the wire. Repeat with the other ribbons.

4 Tape together a length of green florist's wire with 7 stamens using florist's tape. As the tape is pulled taut it becomes self-adhesive. Wrap the tape around the stamens all the way to the end of the wire for stability. Repeat twice more (you will need one for each amaryllis flower).

5 Prepare 6 amaryllis petals for each flower. Using the veining rolling pin, thinly roll out the remaining white gum paste. Place the amaryllis cutter on the paste with the thick vein in the center and cut out 6 petals. Insert approximately ¾ inch of a length of white florist's wire into the thick vein as shown. Lay the wired petal inside the veining mold with the wire facing outwards and firmly press the mold sides together to indent the markings on the petal. Use a ball tool over a foam pad to gently feather the edges of the petal. Allow the petals to dry overnight propped over an upturned bowl or cylindrical tube so that they gently curve backwards.

6 Paint the center length of each petal with green dusting powder.

7 Tape the first 3 petals evenly around the central stamens using florist's tape. Add the final 3 petals one at a time and secure with florist's tape. Finally, tape 1 gold and 2 white ribbon loops at even intervals around each of the finished amaryllis using green florist's tape.

To assemble Fill a small pastry bag with white royal icing and snip the top with sharp scissors. Fix the wide white ribbon around the cake and overlay it with the thin gold ribbon, securing both at the back with royal icing. Glue the thin white ribbon around the baseboard. Remove the sponge from the leaves and secure them into position on the cake with icing. Push the posy pick into the center of the cake until it is flush with the top. Pipe royal icing into the posy pick and gently insert the 3 amaryllis and ribbon loops. Trim the ribbon ends as necessary.

6

7

Tip These fondant amaryllis are extremely fragile! Handle the petals at the bottom where the wire is inserted as this is the most stable point and prepare extra petals for each flower – if one snaps it can be pulled out and another taped into position.

christmas tree

you will need

8-inch oval cake covered with marzipan and purple fondant

3½ oz. white fondant

3½ oz. white gum paste

rolling pin

1-, 2- and 3-inch star cutters

2 oz. white royal icing

pastry bag

silver dragées

40-inch length of star ribbon

For a more contemporary Christmas cake, I have covered this oval-shaped cake with a regal purple fondant. The white Christmas tree is made from a stack of white stars in different sizes studded with silver dragées. To complement the cake I have used a white star ribbon.

Tip Using an equal mixture of fondant and gum paste to make the stars for the Christmas tree will give the finished tree strength and allow it to set firmly more quickly.

1 Combine the fondant and gum paste together and knead until smooth and pliable. Roll out to a thickness of ⅛ inch. Cut out 2 or 3 stars of each size.

2 Starting with the largest stars, pipe a small amount of royal icing in the center of each and stack the next one on top at a slight angle. Repeat until the tree is approximately 6 inches high, using 8–10 stars.

To assemble Place the final star upright on top of the tree as shown. Fix the tree into position on the top of the cake and add silver dragées using royal icing. Tie the star ribbon around the cake.

individual christmas cakes

you will need

2-inch round cakes covered with marzipan and white fondant

green, red and white gum paste

rolling pin

white royal icing

templates (see page 150), optional

tracing paper (optional)

scribe

pastry bags

no. 1.5, no. 2 and no. 5 tips

red, brown, black, yellow, ivory and peach edible food colors

holly cutter

Christmas tree cutter

paintbrush

gold luster

alcohol dipping solution

¼-inch width red ribbon to fix around the bottom of each cake

These adorable individual Christmas cakes are such fun to make and they make the most wonderful stocking fillers. I have also used them, presented in clear boxes tied with a ribbon, as place settings for the Christmas table. Although I have provided a template for the angel and reindeer, try piping these freehand once you have built up confidence so each character is unique.

1 To make the Santa hat, form a piece of red gum paste into a cone and fold the top over gently. Roll out a ball of white gum paste and gently press this between your thumb and forefinger to create a flattened disk. Press the red cone onto the white bottom. Cut the hat in half vertically and fix into position on the cake with royal icing. Make a white ball of gum paste for the bobble and fix in place.

2 Trace the reindeer template on page 150 onto a piece of tracing paper, lay it onto the cake and use a scribe to gently transfer the shape onto the cake. Pipe the outline onto the cake using white royal icing and a no 1.5 tip. Flood the face and antlers with brown icing. When the icing is dry, pipe on 2 white eyes, using a no. 2 tip, 2 black pupils and a large red nose.

3 To make the holly and berries, roll out the green gum paste very thinly and cut out 3 holly leaves. Curl the leaves very gently and ice them into position on the cake. Roll a piece of red gum paste into 3 small balls to make the berries and fix these into position with royal icing.

4 For the Christmas tree, roll out the green gum paste very thinly and cut out a Christmas tree shape. Ice into position on the cake. Pipe a white star on the top of the tree using a no. 5 tip and 5 red baubles using a no. 1.5 tip.

5 Transfer the angel template on page 150 onto the cake. Pipe around the outline of the shape using white royal icing and a no. 1.5 tip. Mix a small amount of ivory and peach colored icing together to create a skin color and use to flood the face and feet. Flood the hair and pipe a halo in golden yellow and flood the wings white. Allow to dry, then using a paintbrush and food color, add the facial details. Luster the hair and halo with gold luster powder. Finally, fix a length of ribbon around the base of each cake, securing it at the back with royal icing.

christmas package

you will need

2 (6-inch) square cakes stacked together with apricot jam or buttercream

pastry brush

apricot jam

3 lb. 14 oz. marzipan

brandy

5 lb. red fondant

confectioners' sugar

rolling pin

ruler

sharp knife

7-inch square piece of paper

3½ oz. white fondant

1½-inch star cutter

waxed paper

sugar glue

edible glitter

8-ft. length of colorful wired ribbon

royal iciing

9-inch square board covered with red fondant and edged with 40-inch length of ⅝-inch wide red ribbon

This cake has been made to look like a tantalizing Christmas present box. It is a versatile design that can be adapted for many occasions by changing the colors and ribbon. The cake is very deep, made up of two 6-inch square cakes to form a cube.

1 Brush the cake with boiled apricot jam and cover with marzipan in panels as though it were to be covered with royal icing. (This will give the box squarer edges.) Brush the sides of the cake with brandy. Knead the red fondant until smooth and pliable and divide into 3 equal portions. Lightly dust a work surface with confectioners' sugar and roll out two-thirds of the fondant into a large rectangle. Use a ruler and cut a fat strip large enough to fit around the 4 sides of the box in one piece. Use a knife to trim the icing so it is flush with the top of the cake. Roll out the remaining one-third of the fondant and cut out a 10-inch square. Lay a 7-inch square piece of paper in the center (to allow for depth of marzipan and icing) and trim away the 4 corners as shown to form the box lid.

2 Brush the cake top with brandy and place the lid into position pinching the corners to neaten. Trim the overhang with a knife if necessary.

3 Knead the white fondant until smooth and pliable. Lightly dust a work surface with confectioners' sugar and roll out the paste to a thickness of ⅛ inch. Cut out several white stars and allow to dry.

4 Place the stars onto a clean sheet of waxed paper. Brush with sugar glue and pour edible glitter over the top.

5 Cut the wired ribbon in half. Lay the 2 pieces across one another to form a large cross. Sit the cake centrally on top. Draw the 4 edges of the ribbon up and tie into a bow on the top. Fix the stars into position on the cake with royal icing. Fix the cake into position on the iced board.

Tip This cake works as a maximum 6-inch height box. Any deeper and the cake will be too heavy to support itself. If you want to make the cake larger, use a larger square pan, but keep to this height.

winter igloo

you will need

10-inch round cake covered with marzipan and white fondant

5-inch dome cake (use one half of a ball sphere pan) covered with marzipan and white fondant

16-inch round board covered with white fondant

marking tool

white, black, red, blue and orange modeling paste

paintbrush

sugar glue

pastry bags

no. 1.5 and no. 2 tips

white and black royal icing

piping gel

3-ft. length of 1-inch width white ribbon for the cake

3-ft. length of ⅝-inch width light blue ribbon for the cake

white hologram edible glitter

5-ft. length of ⅝-inch width white ribbon to edge the baseboard

glue stick (to fix ribbon around baseboard)

This cake was originally designed for a very special girl's third birthday. The cute polar bears and penguins are made from modeling paste, although the igloo is a real cake. Why not make the bottom cake one flavor and have the igloo as another flavor – just for the birthday person? Dust the snowballs with glitter and the tongues and noses of the polar bears with piping gel for authenticity.

1 With a marking tool score concentric circles around the igloo working upwards. Mark vertical lines to represent bricks. Make the entrance of the igloo from a sausage of white modeling paste, slightly hollowed out at one end, and square the sides gently. Score the bricks using the marking tool.

2 Mold modeling paste into the various parts of the polar bear as shown: white for the polar bear's body and ears and squares for the scarf; red for the scarf and tongue and black for the nose.

3 Attach the ears, nose and tongue onto the head, and squares onto the scarf, with sugar glue. Brush the back of the scarf with sugar glue and wrap around the polar bear. Pipe eyes using white royal icing with a no. 2 tip, followed by a black pupil with a no. 1.5 tip. Brush the nose and tongue with piping gel to create a glistening wet effect.

4 To make the penguin, mold black modeling paste into body shape and 2 wings. Use white paste to make the front of the body and a scarf, orange for the feet and beak and blue for the squares on scarf.

5 Use sugar glue to fix the front of the body onto the black body shape and to attach wings to shoulders. Flatten the ends of the wings so they sit away from the body. Fix feet, beak and scarf in position with sugar glue. Use black royal icing and a no. 2 tip to pipe 2 eyes.

To assemble Offset the cake on the lined board and fix the wider white ribbon, overlaid with the blue ribbon, around it. Secure the igloo, igloo entrance, penguins and polar bears in position on top of the cake with royal icing. Make snowballs from white modeling paste and ice them into place on the cake. Brush them with sugar glue then with white hologram glitter. Use the narrower white ribbon to edge the baseboard.

building blocks

you will need

2-inch cake cubes, covered with marzipan and white, pink or blue fondant

pink and blue fondant for polka dots

sugar glue

paintbrush

white sugar rosebuds (see page 87)

white royal icing

pastry bag

no. 1.5 and no. 3 piping tips

½-inch width white, pink and blue ribbon

white, light blue, dark blue, light brown, dark brown and pink modeling paste

dried spaghetti

star-marking tool

brown liquid food coloring

4-tier iced stand—8-, 10-, 12- and 14-inch boards edged with ⅝-inch width ribbon and polystyrene blocks wrapped with 1-inch width ribbon

½-inch cubes of fondant

Individual building-block cakes are a lovely idea for a child's christening or first birthday. I have made this cake in shades of blue and pink with a model of a teddy bear and his train on the top – change the color of the fondant on the cakes or mold another sugar toy on the top to personalize the design. The little building blocks are made from colored fondant and are presented on a purpose-built stand, adding height and drama to the cake.

1 Cover some of the white cakes with polka dots made from tiny flattened balls of pink or blue fondant fixed in position on the cakes with sugar glue.

2 Attach a white sugar rosebud (see page 87) to each of the remaining white cakes using royal icing. Pipe letters or numbers onto the pink and blue cakes using the no. 3 tip. Fix ribbon around the bottom of each cake, holding it in position at the back with royal icing.

3 Shape a body for the teddy bear from white modeling paste and insert a strand of dried spaghetti to protrude from the top. Mark stars on the body using the star-marking tool. Following the picture, make arms, slippers and a hat from dark blue paste; collar, cuffs, hat brim and pompom from pale blue paste; head, ear, hands and feet from dark brown paste and a face from the light brown paste.

4 Using sugar glue, attach arms, cuffs, hands, feet and shoes to the body, and ear and face to the head. Thread the collar onto the body, then secure the head. Attach the brim and pompom to the hat. Insert a strand of spaghetti into the head to support the hat and thread it on. Paint eyes, nose and mouth with brown food color.

5 Make 12 train wheels from white modeling paste and mold white, blue and pink blocks as shown. Fix all pieces together with sugar glue to form the engine and 2 carriages.

To assemble Position the individual cakes onto the stand starting with the bottom tier and working upwards. Fill a pastry bag with a no. 1.5 tip and fresh white royal icing and ice the teddy bear into position on the top board together with the train set and ½-inch cubes of fondant to resemble building blocks.

birthday clown

you will need

8-inch oval-shaped cake covered with marzipan and purple fondant

11-inch oval board covered with purple fondant

6½-ft. length of colorful wired ribbon to tie around the cake

template (see page 150)

tracing paper

waxed paper

masking tape

pastry bags

no 1.5 tip

5½ oz. white royal icing

red, yellow, blue, green and black edible food colors

paintbrush

yellow, green and blue fondant

star cutter

40-inch length of ⅜-inch width purple ribbon to fix around the board

glue stick (to fix ribbon around board)

chocolate drops (optional)

Children's birthday parties tend to conjure up images of painted faces, party games, balloons, streamers, toys and a special birthday cake. It is becoming common for children to have themed parties, sometimes with professional entertainers, and clowns are a particularly popular choice. This cake would complement such an occasion very well. I have added some brightly colored chocolate drops around the cake for those too impatient to wait until the candles have been blown out!

 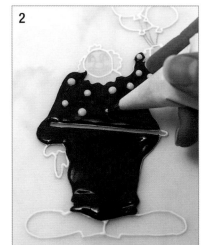

1 Position the cake centrally onto the board. Fix the ribbon around the bottom of the cake and tie with a bow. Transfer the template on page 150 onto tracing paper. On a flat work surface, fix a sheet of waxed paper over the design and secure with masking tape. Fill a pastry bag with a no. 1.5 tip and white royal icing and pipe around the clown template as shown. Do not pipe the balloon strings or the clown's facial features.

2 Place 1 tablespoon of royal icing into each of 4 bowls and thin with a little water to create flooding icing. Color the icing in one bowl red, one yellow, one green and one blue. Fill a pastry bag with red flooding icing, snip the end and flood the clown's body. Before it has had time to set,

fill a second pastry bag with a no. 1.5 tip and yellow flooding icing and drop yellow spots into position using a paintbrush so they merge into the red. Continue to flood sections of the clown, allowing time for the icing to form a crust before flooding adjoining sections. Allow to dry overnight. Pipe the facial features and black detail with royal icing.

To assemble Carefully peel the waxed paper away from the clown and fix the clown into position on the cake with royal icing. Pipe balloon strings with black royal icing. Roll out the colored fondant, stamp out some stars and fix into position on the cake and board. Edge the board with narrow ribbon and, if you wish, dress the table with hand-decorated chocolate drops.

teddy bear christening

you will need

8-inch petal-shaped cake covered with marzipan and yellow fondant

8-, 11- and 12-inch petal-shaped boards, largest only covered with yellow fondant

scribe

3½ oz. white royal icing

2 pastry bags

no. 1.5 and no. 3 tips

9 oz. white modeling paste

light brown, dark brown and yellow edible food coloring

dried spaghetti

marking tools

small rolling pin

flower stamps (small and medium)

sugar glue

2 oz. royal icing – white and black

4-ft. length of ⅝-inch width white ribbon to fix around 12-inch baseboard

glue stick (to fix ribbon around board)

One of the very first cakes I made was a christening cake for my god-daughter Hannah. It, too, was a delicate petal-shaped cake dressed with yellow and white. Here I have added a pretty 'needlepoint' design around the top edge of the cake, which is mirrored around the board. The cake is finished with a plump sugar teddy bear holding a building block.

1 Place the 11-inch board centrally over the 12-inch covered board and scribe around the outside. Position the cake centrally onto the covered board and fix into position with royal icing. Place the 8-inch board centrally over the cake and scribe around the outside. Using a no. 3 tip and white royal icing, pipe a trail of pearls around the bottom of the cake. Using a no. 1.5 tip, pipe the picot and heart design around the top of the cake and the cake board as shown. Keep the 2 lobes of the heart and the double picot pearls on the scribed line as you work around.

2 To make the teddy bear, divide the modeling paste into 5 equal balls and color 2 light brown, 1 dark brown and 1 yellow. With the light brown paste make the body, arms, feet and circles for the face. Insert a piece of dried spaghetti so it protrudes 1 inch out of the top of the body. Make the ribbons, bow and small building block with the yellow modeling paste; the head, ears and nose from dark brown paste; and the dress from white paste, as shown. Roll out a small amount of paste thinly and stamp out 16–18 yellow or white small flowers.

3 Place the dress over the body and gently fold the bottom to create movement. Attach all elements of the body and clothes as shown, using sugar glue. Use royal icing to pipe the eyes and fix the small flowers into position around the top edge of the teddy's dress and by one ear. Pipe a letter on the building block and pipe the centers of all the flowers.

To assemble Fix the teddy bear on the cake with royal icing and add a few cut-out flowers in various colors and sizes. Pipe the 'AaBbCc' on the cake and attach ribbon to the board.

easter cookies

These cute Easter cookies – chicks, butterflies and flowers – are brightly decorated with fondant and royal icing. They make lovely gifts presented in a clear bag tied with a pretty ribbon.

christmas cookies

you will need

1 recipe of spiced cookie dough (see page 21)

shaped cookie cutters

fondant

brown and green edible food colors

rolling pin

confectioners' sugar

colored royal icing

pastry bags

tips

clear cellophane bags

ribbon

Christmas is a time for giving and these hand-decorated spiced cookies make wonderful gifts presented in clear cellophane bags or gift boxes tied with a red ribbon. Alternatively, make a hole in the top of the cookies with a straw before they are baked and hang the decorated cookies with ribbon on your Christmas tree. These cookies are fun to make with children and make great presents for grandparents and school teachers.

1 Stamp out shapes from a batch of cookie dough using cutters in Christmas shapes – reindeers, Christmas trees, holly, stars and angels. Bake the cookies following the instructions on page 21. Color some fondant brown for reindeers and green for trees and holly, leaving some white for stars and angels. Knead the fondant until smooth and pliable and roll out to a thickness of ⅛ inch on a work surface lightly dusted with confectioners' sugar. Use the cookie cutter to cut out the fondant and fix it into position on the cookie with royal icing.

2 Use colored royal icing to pipe decorations onto the fondant-topped cookies. For the reindeers, pipe black antlers, a white eye and black pupil, and a large red nose.

3 Christmas trees can be decorated with red "baubles" and a white star, using a star tip. Allow the cookies to dry before wrapping them in clear cellophane bags and tying with ribbon. The cookies will remain fresh for 7 days if kept in an airtight container.

signature cakes

signature style

The cakes in this section are all firm favorites from my personal portfolio. Each has been inspired, designed and created to reflect my clean, classical, contemporary style. I have been allowed to indulge my passion here and present a collection of beautifully romantic, flawless jewels with exceptional attention to detail. Several of these designs are based on exquisite jewelry, including the Fabergé and black-pearl tiara. You could personalize your own cake by adapting the design of a family heirloom, tiara, necklace or brooch. Many of these cakes can be adapted in size, shape and color to complement your special occasion so you may create your own spectacular cake.

1950s chic

you will need

3-tier square cake—4-, 6- and 8-inch tiers covered with marzipan and white royal icing, placed on boards 3 inches larger than each tier covered with white royal icing

pastry bag

no. 3 tip

7 oz. white royal icing

2 polystyrene blocks (4 inches smaller than the middle and bottom tiers)

fresh, wired flowers to dress

8 dowels

5-ft. length of ⅜-inch width white ribbon to edge the boards

glue stick (to fix ribbon around boards)

This 1950s chic design – one of my favorite wedding cakes – was inspired by style icons of an era that has popular appeal today. The square tiers are royal iced to achieve clean sharp edges that are then hand piped with a pinstripe design in white royal icing. I have finished each tier with a row of royal-iced pearls around the top and bottom edge then blocked the wedding cake with fresh white roses and paper white narcissi.

Fill a pastry bag with no. 3 tip and white royal icing and pipe vertical lines at equal distances around each tier. Pipe a trail of pearls around the top and bottom edge of each tier and allow to dry.

To assemble Stud the polystyrene blocks with fresh, wired flowers (see page 53). Stack the tiers by inserting dowels (with a gentle boring motion to avoid cracking the icing), following instructions on page 34. Finally, edge the boards with white ribbon.

cascading lily

you will need

3-tier round cake—6-, 9- and 12-inch tiers covered with marzipan and white fondant and stacked centrally on a 16-inch round board covered with white fondant

24-gauge wires, each cut into 3 equal lengths

white gum paste

paintbrush

green dusting powder

large white lily stamens

green florist's tape

small veining rolling pin

4-inch lily cutter

26-gauge wires, each cut into 3 equal lengths

4-inch lily-veining mold

ball tool

soft foam pad

pink dusting powder

brown liquid food coloring

8-ft. length of ½-inch width ivory ribbon

5-ft. length of ⅝-inch width ivory ribbon

5½ oz. white royal icing

pastry bag and no. 3 tip

12 posy picks

white wire curls made with 28-gauge wire

I like the fresh, clean feel of this stacked cake, which has been decorated with hand-piped cascading pearls and dressed with handmade sugar lilies. The wire curls are made by twisting a length of 28-gauge wire around a single dowel. By changing the colors of the lilies this cake can be adapted to complement your wedding, or can be used for a single-tier anniversary cake.

Tip You will need 6 petals for each lily but as they're very fragile, it is a good idea to make extra. If a petal snaps, pull it out gently and tape another into position.

1 Bend the top of a 24-gauge wire over to form a small hook. Form white gum paste into an elongated cone, pinch the blunt end into 3 and mark with a cross. Insert the hooked end of the wire gently into the thin end of the cone and allow to dry overnight before brushing with green dusting powder. Position 6 large lily stamens around the center and tape into position with green florist's tape.

2 Roll out the white gum paste thinly using the veining rolling pin. Place the lily cutter on the paste with the thick vein in the center and cut out 6 petals. Insert approximately ¾ inch of a 26-gauge wire into the thick vein of each petal. Lay the wired petal inside the veining mold with the wire facing outwards and firmly press the mold sides together to indent the markings on the petal. Use a ball tool over a foam pad to gently feather the edges of the lily.

3 Allow the lily petals to dry overnight propped over an upturned bowl so that the petals gently curve backwards. (For a more closed lily dry the petals flat.) Dust the center length of each petal with pink dusting powder and use a paintbrush dipped into brown liquid food coloring to paint small dots on top. Allow to dry.

4 Tape the first 3 petals evenly around the central stamens using florist's tape. Add the final 3 petals one at a time and fix in position with tape. Handle the lilies at the bottom where the wire is inserted as this is the most stable point.

To assemble Secure lengths of narrower ribbon around each tier and wider ribbon round the baseboard, fixing at the back with royal icing. Starting with the top tier and working downwards, pipe random pearls, concentrating them at the bottom of each tier, as shown. Use a clean paintbrush to remove the point of each pearl and leave the cake to dry overnight. Push the posy picks into the cake at intervals, fill them with royal icing and insert the sugar flowers and wire curls into each.

corsage rose

you will need

8-inch round cake covered with marzipan and fondant and placed offset onto a 12-inch board covered with fondant

24-gauge wires

green florist's tape

deep red gum paste

small rolling pin

1½-, 2- and 3-inch rose cutters

ball tool

soft foam pad

paintbrush

sugar glue

pale pink gum paste

forest-green gum paste

2½-inch calyx cutter

1½- and 2-inch rose-leaf cutters

3-ft. length of 1¼-inch width fuchsia-pink ribbon

6½-ft. length of ⅝-inch width red ribbon

pastry bag and no.1.5 tip

2 oz. royal icing

50 small silver ball dragées

6½-ft. total length of ½-inch width ribbon in shades of red and pink made into 5 triple ribbon bows

5 green wire curls made with 28-gauge wire (see page 121)

2 posy picks

This vintage cake design was originally commissioned by *Vogue* magazine after I had designed the wedding cake for Madonna and Guy Ritchie. Inspired by blousy corsage fabric roses, it is dressed with handmade oversized sugar roses. Although I have chosen here to decorate a single tier, this design transposes well for an elegant wedding cake. Make roses in shades of antique ivory and caramel and use them to decorate a tiered, stacked, royal-iced cake.

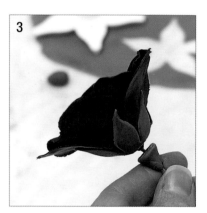

1 Cut one 24-gauge wire into 4 equal lengths and tape them together using florist's tape. Bend the top ⅛ inch over to create a hook. Taper a cone shape of hazelnut-sized red gum paste onto the hooked wire. Allow to dry and firm overnight.

2 Roll out a small piece of red gum paste and cut out a small rose shape. Use a ball tool over a foam pad to gently curve each petal. Brush a small amount of sugar glue in the center of the rose and thread the wire through the center. Gently fold petals up and around the cone to create a delicate rose bud. Allow to set overnight. Repeat to make 2 roses with the 2-inch cutter and 2 with the 3-inch cutter, some from pink gum paste.

3 Roll out the green paste very thinly and cut out a calyx shape using a 2½-inch calyx cutter. Use the ball tool over a soft pad to gently shape each of the calyx strands. Brush the calyx with sugar glue and thread the rose onto the calyx. Gently press a small cone of green paste into position for stability. Make leaves from green gum paste following the instructions for making lily petals on page 121.

To assemble Fix the wide fuchsia ribbon around the cake and overlay it with the narrower red ribbon. Edge the board with red ribbon. Using a pastry bag with a no. 1.5 tip and white royal icing, attach the silver balls randomly around the cake. Arrange together a selection of roses, leaves, ribbon loops and wire curls using florist's tape. Insert the posy picks into the cake, fill with icing and insert the flower sprays.

butterflies

you will need

4-tier round cake—4-, 6-, 8- and 10-inch tiers covered with white fondant, stacked centrally and placed on 13-inch and 16-inch boards covered with white fondant

23-ft. length of ⅝-inch width white ribbon

butterfly template (see page 151)

tracing paper

waxed paper

masking tape

pastry bags

no. 1.5 and no. 3 tips

18 oz. white royal icing (yields 16–20 butterflies)

buttercup yellow and leaf green food colors

paintbrush

wooden pick

sponge cut into ⅜-inch cubes (or cotton balls)

20 flower stamens, cut in half

2 oz. gum paste

1-inch calyx cutter

ball tool and foam pad

These delicate sugar butterflies epitomize summer without the use of flowers. Made from royal icing in a run-out technique, they can be a mass of bright colors or in soft pastels. They can be used to dress wedding, birthday or christening cakes or iced into position on individual cakes. Little cakes can be presented in a clear box finished with a ribbon for guests to take home as favors.

1 Fix lengths of ribbon around each tier and around the baseboards. Trace a selection of butterfly designs (see page 151) onto tracing paper and fix a piece of waxed paper, shiny side up, over the top, holding both in position with masking tape. Using a no. 1.5 tip and white royal icing, pipe the outline.

2 Reserve 2 large tablespoons of royal icing and thin remainder with water as flooding icing. Separate into 3 bowls, color one yellow and one green. Fill 3 pastry bags with icing and flood butterflies. Use a small damp paintbrush to pull the icing to fill all the corners.

3 While the icing is still wet, add detail with the other colors inside the wings and drag with a wooden pick to form patterns. Allow to set for 15 minutes then flood the lower wings. Leave the iced butterfy wings overnight to dry .

4 Peel the butterfly wings from the waxed paper. Fill a pastry bag with a no. 3 tip and reserved royal icing. Pipe a head and body onto clean waxed paper and then attach wings onto the iced body at an angle, supporting each one with a small piece of sponge (or cotton ball). Insert 2 stamens for antennae. Leave to dry overnight.

To assemble Cut out tiny flowers from white gum paste using a calyx cutter. Form with a ball tool over a foam pad. Allow to dry. Fix butterflies and flowers onto the cake with icing. Pipe flower centers with yellow icing.

fleur-de-lis

you will need

4-tier round cake—6-, 8-, 10- and 12-inch tiers covered with marzipan and ivory fondant

15-inch round board covered with ivory fondant

template (see page 151)

waxed paper

pen

masking tape

scribe

pastry bag fitted with no. 2 tip

7 oz. white royal icing

topaz luster

edible gel

paintbrush

10-ft. length of ½-inch width ivory ribbon to fix around the base of each tier

5-ft. length of ⅝-inch width ivory ribbon for the board

This is a smaller replica of the six-tier wedding cake I created for Pierce Brosnan and Keely Shaye Smith. The tiers are stacked and I have dressed the cake here with fresh apricot amaryllis and delicate white sweet peas. The design is repeated three times symmetrically around each tier. As the circumference will change for every cake it is impossible to provide one definitive template. Follow the instructions given on page 151 to ensure that the design lines up perfectly on each tier.

1 Transfer the template on page 151 onto waxed paper and fix around the cake, holding in position with masking tape. Use a scribe to prick the design onto the cake.

2 Fill a pastry bag with a no. 2 tip and white royal icing. Pipe the design as shown, including all the pearls. Allow to dry. Blend ½ teaspoon of topaz luster with 1 teaspoon edible gel and glaze each pearl using a paintbrush.

To assemble Allow each tier to dry before stacking the tiers centrally. Finish by wrapping the narrower ribbon around the base of each tier and the wider ribbon around the baseboard, securing it at the back of the cake with royal icing.

contemporary romantic

I find the clean, simple lines of this contemporary cake aesthetically pleasing and it has proved to be a firm favorite with many others too. After it was featured in a bridal magazine in the UK, I received more calls than I have for any other cake. However, because it is so simple, it needs to be precision perfect with hidden construction.

you will need

4-tier square cake—6-, 8-, 10- and 12-inch tiers placed on boards the same size and covered (to the base of each board) with marzipan and ivory fondant

4 boards, 3 inches larger than each cake tier (for transporting the cakes only)

3 (2-inch deep) square polystyrene blocks—4-, 5- and 6-inch

12 dowels

60 fresh, wired roses ('Blue Curioso') to dress

metal spatula

Carefully set the tiers down onto plain boards 3 inches larger to dry and allow for transportation. Position the polystyrene blocks and insert the dowels (see page 34). Block each tier with fresh, wired roses (see page 53) before you attempt to assemble the cake.

To assemble Because the tiers are on hidden boards, you'll need to handle the cakes with extreme care to avoid damaging the icing around the bottom. Gently move the cake to the edge of the protective board using a metal spatula to loosen the cake and allow you to grasp it from underneath. Repeat with other tiers.

aroma romantic

This is an adaptation of the contemporary romantic wedding cake shown opposite. I have added a wide ribbon around the base of a two-tier hexagonal cake, which can mask an unsightly edge, and have finished the cake by randomly hand piping tiny pearls on each tier. The cake has been blocked with fresh aromatic roses.

you will need

2-tier hexagonal cake—9- and 12-inch tiers placed on boards the same size and covered (to the base of each board) with marzipan and ivory fondant

2 boards, 3 inches larger than cake tiers (for transporting the cakes only)

6½-ft. length of 1-inch width ivory satin ribbon

2 oz. royal icing

pastry bag

no. 1.5 tip

4 dowels

6-inch round x 2-inch deep polystyrene block

20 fresh, wired roses ('Aroma') to dress

metal spatula

Carefully set the tiers down onto plain boards 3 inches larger to dry and allow for transportation. Fix lengths of ribbon around the base of each tier and fix in position with royal icing. Pipe random pearls on each tier using a no. 1.5 tip.

To assemble Insert the dowels and position the polystyrene block (see page 34). Block the bottom tier with fresh, wired roses (see page 53). Gently move the 9-inch cake to the edge of the protective board using a metal spatula to loosen the cake and allow you to grasp it from underneath. Set the cake over the bottom tier and dress the top of the cake with fresh roses.

Fabergé

you will need

6-inch square cake covered with marzipan and ivory fondant

template (see page 152)

waxed paper

pen

ruler

scribe

½-inch width ribbon to fix around the base of the cake

3½ oz. white royal icing

pastry bags

no. 3 and no. 1.5 tips

topaz luster

edible gel

paintbrush

fresh flowers to dress

I was inspired to create this cake after visiting a tiara exhibition held at London's Victoria and Albert Museum. Based on an original Fabergé tiara, this traditional-looking cake will suit the most formal of occasions. The design lends itself to a round or square cake as it is repeated four times around each tier. Piping it in white creates an alabaster feel while elements of the pearls are glazed so the cake shimmers.

1 Trace the template onto waxed paper. Hold the template centrally against the side of the cake (use a ruler to measure the center accurately and line the top pearl with this mark) and use a scribe to prick the design through. Fix the ribbon around the bottom, securing it with royal icing at the back.

2 Fill 2 separate pastry bags with a no. 3 and no. 1.5 tip and white royal icing. Using the no. 3 tip, pipe the main design, including all the large pearls and pearl drop.

3 Surround the central pearl drop and 2 outer pearls with tiny pearls using the no. 1.5 tip as shown. Repeat on all 4 sides and allow to dry.

4 Blend ½ teaspoon of topaz luster with 1 teaspoon of edible gel and glaze each of the large pearls using a paintbrush as shown. Allow the icing to dry, then dress the top of the cake with fresh flowers.

4-tier Wedgewood-blue Fabergé

This impressive 4-tier round cake has been covered with Wedgewood-blue fondant, with the Fabergé design piped in white. For a round cake you will need to measure the circumference accurately using ribbon (see page 152). I have placed each tier on a board 3 inches larger than the cake, then blocked the tiers with purple roses and offset each tier.

vanity fair

you will need

3-tier cake covered with marzipan and pink fondant placed on boards 3 inches larger than each tier, covered with pink fondant

baseboard 6 inches larger than the bottom tier, covered with pink fondant

3 boards the same size as the cakes

scribe

royal icing

pastry bags and no. 1.5 and no. 3 tips

template (see page 154), optional

paintbrush

clear piping gel or topaz luster mixed with alcohol dipping solution

⅝-inch width ribbon for cakes

1-inch width ribbon for boards

glue stick

grid template (see page 146)

6 dowels

6 (3½-inch) pillars

pen

ruler

sharp heavy-duty scissors or a small hacksaw

This design is relatively simple to achieve, yet the end result is effective and elegant. The pearls are hand piped around the top edge of the cake and a simple wide ribbon wrapped around the bottom. The design works particularly well with contrasting colors and equally well with different-shaped cakes.

1 Position a cake board the same size as each cake carefully on each cake top and scribe around each. Lift the boards off and gently brush away any excess icing. Using a no. 3 tip, pipe a single row of large pearls directly over the scribed template marked on the top of each cake. Following the picture, or using the template on page 154, create hanging strands of pearls. Use a no. 1.5 tip for the smaller pearls and a no. 3 tip for the larger ones. Once the icing is dry, the pearls can be brushed with a glaze — use either clear piping gel or topaz luster mixed with alcohol dipping solution.

To assemble Fix lengths of the narrower ribbon around each tier and the wider ribbon around the boards. Assemble the tiers following the instructions given on page 36.

4-tier taupe vanity fair

In addition to the pearls around the top lip of each tier, I have included tiny random pearls, piped with a no. 1.5 tip, to the sides of this cake. Resplendent and rather regal, this 4-tier stacked cake is beautifully accompanied by the rich, warm colors of silk anemones. Stack the cake (see page 35) after you have decorated and lustered each tier.

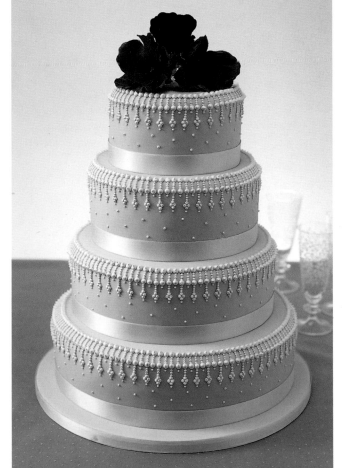

art deco

you will need

3-tier cake—4-, 6- and 8-inch tiers, covered with marzipan and royal icing

3 boards—3 inches larger than each cake tier, covered with icing

template (see page 153)

masking tape

heavy-duty waxed paper

pastry bags and no. 1.5 tip

4 lb. 8 oz. royal icing (and extra egg white)

mint-green and gray edible food coloring

paintbrush

silver luster

alcohol dipping solution

small offset spatula

ruler

scribe

⅝-inch width ribbon to edge boards

½-inch width ribbon to fix around cakes

I have had the honored experience of working with the most prestigious hotels and venues in London. One of my favorite hotels is Claridge's and its architecture, furnishings and colors provided the inspiration for this Art Deco-style cake. Although this is a very stylish design, every panel is a labor of love – allow at least 10 hours to make all 36 panels required (plus a few spares) for this cake.

size of square cake	number of panels required
4-inch	2 each side, 8 total
6-inch	3 each side, 12 total
8-inch	4 each side, 16 total
10-inch	5 each side, 20 total
12-inch	6 each side, 24 total
14-inch	7 each side, 28 total
16-inch	8 each side, 32 total

The template for this cake works for cakes baked in even sizes, but does not lend itself to cakes baked in odd sizes (i.e. 7-inch, 9-inch, 11-inch, etc.).

Tip On the top and bottom tiers, which have an even number of panels, arrange the first side quickly and line up into position by gently sliding the panels. On the middle tier, position the central panel first and work outwards.

1 Begin with all cakes covered and positioned on the iced boards. To make the royal-iced Art Deco panels, place photocopies of the template on page 153 onto a clean work surface that can be left undisturbed overnight and fix into position with masking tape. Place sheets of waxed paper over the top (shiny side up) and fix with masking tape. Using a pastry bag fitted with a no. 1.5 tip and filled with royal icing, pipe the outline of each panel, ensuring the lines are straight and even.

2 Thin the remainder of the royal icing down with fresh egg white to a runnier consistency as the flooding icing (see page 28). Separate this into 3 equal parts. Color one-third mint green and another light gray. Fill a pastry bag with the white flooding icing and snip the very end of the bag with sharp scissors. Flood all the left-hand center section using a paintbrush to pull and push the icing neatly into the corners. By the time

you have repeated the above for all panels, the icing should have formed enough of a skin to allow you to flood the right-hand center section. Repeat for all panels.

3 Fill another pastry bag with the mint-green icing and flood both side wings on each panel. Because they are not directly touching each other it is fine to flood both before moving on to the next panel.

4 Fill a third pastry bag with the gray icing and flood all the bottom triangles. Allow to dry overnight. Brush the bottom triangles with silver luster mixed with alcohol dipping solution. I have found it more effective to quickly apply 2 thin coats rather than brush a single thick coat. These panels can be made in advance and carefully stored in a cake box layered with paper towels. Be careful though as the silver dust rubs off very easily once the alcohol has evaporated.

To assemble Peel the panels from the waxed paper using a small offset spatula. Pipe a small amount of icing onto the back of each panel and place into position on the cake. Use a ruler to scribe a double line around the board of each tier. Using a no. 1.5 tip, pipe gray royal icing over the 2 scribed lines and add evenly spaced curved 'C's all facing the same way. Allow to dry before brushing with silver luster dissolved in alcohol dipping solution. Edge boards and cakes with ribbon and tier the cake as shown on page 36.

strawberry helter-skelter

you will need

10-inch cake covered with white chocolate plastic

13-inch and 16-inch boards covered with white chocolate plastic

18 oz. tempered white chocolate, melted

5 dowels

heavy-duty scissors or a small hacksaw

8-inch round board

8-inch diameter x 12-inch high polystyrene cone

paintbrush

3½ lb. white chocolate plastic

rolling pin

confectioners' sugar

2½ lb. strawberries

tempered white chocolate for dipping

waxed paper

⅝-inch width cream grosgrain ribbon to edge boards

This white chocolate helter-skelter makes a fantastic centerpiece for a very special occasion. Because I have used a polystyrene cone placed on top of a real cake, the finished helter-skelter can be scaled up for even more dramatic effect – I once made a five-foot high one! This impressive cake is ideal for large social gatherings, but you will need to have enough extra cutting cake for all your guests, beautifully plated and ready to serve, in the kitchen.

Tip This cake looks equally impressive when made with dark chocolate plastic and dressed with a mix of soft fruits and berries. See the picture on page 2.

1 Place the chocolate-covered cake onto the baseboards and secure into position with melted chocolate or royal icing. Insert the dowels and cut flush to the top of the cake (see page 34). Use melted chocolate to stick the 8-inch round board to the bottom of the polystyrene cone. Spread a small amount of melted white chocolate on the top of the cake and fix the cone into position.

2 Paint the sides of the cake and the entire cone with melted white chocolate. Work quickly as the chocolate plastic will need to be wrapped around before the chocolate sets.

3 Knead the white chocolate plastic until smooth and pliable. Divide into 3 and roll out 2 of the pieces on a work surface lightly dusted with confectioners' sugar into 2 long strips, each approximately 24 x 6 inches. Use a sharp knife to neaten the long edges. Feather one long edge of each strip by pressing down on it with a rolling pin using the ball of your palm.

4 Beginning at the bottom of the cone and with the straight edge of the chocolate strip flush with the bottom of the cake, carefully wrap the chocolate around the cake and cone as shown. Repeat with the next strip, creating interesting pockets and shapes as you work upwards and finishing with a flourish. Use the final third of white chocolate plastic to make the fans (see page 76). Fix these into position around the cake with melted white chocolate.

To assemble As long as there is no fresh fruit inside the cake it can remain in this state, stored in a cool dry place (but not refrigerated) for up to 3 days. When you are ready to dress the cake, dip strawberries in tempered white chocolate and allow them to cool and harden on waxed paper. Wrap the ribbon around the baseboards, then arrange the dipped strawberries in the pockets formed around the helter-skelter, adding a few around the baseboard.

black-pearl tiara

you will need

8-inch round cake covered with marzipan and ivory fondant

pen

template (see page 154)

waxed paper

masking tape

scribe

pastry bags

no. 3, no. 2 and no. 1.5 tips

3½ oz. black royal icing

½-inch width ribbon to fix around the base of the cake

fresh flowers and candles to decorate

It is the current fashion for brides to wear beautiful gilded tiaras either with or to replace a lace veil. On this cake, which was inspired by a pearl tiara, I have repeated the pattern around the tier, hand piping pearls of different sizes. This design lends itself to stark contrasting colors, such as black on ivory as used here, or ivory on caramel used on the three-tier cake below. For a truly romantic wedding cake, brush ivory pearls with topaz luster.

1 Trace the template onto a length of waxed paper large enough to fit around the cake (use ribbon to measure). Fix the waxed paper around the cake with masking tape and use a scribe to prick the design onto the cake.

2 Fill 3 separate pastry bags with a no. 3, no. 2 and no. 1.5 tip and black royal icing. Using the no. 3 tip, pipe the single row of pearls around the cake, followed by the single large pearls at intervals at the top and bottom. Use the no. 2 tip to pipe the diamanté designs and the no. 1.5 tip for all the tiny pearls. Allow to dry then fix ribbon around the bottom of the cake and dress the top with fresh flowers and candles.

3-tier caramel tiara

This sophisticated combination of caramel icing with ivory pearls is one option to complement the current trend for taupe or caramel colors in bridal wear. It also works very well with strong flower colors, such as deep reds, purples and pinks. The color is achieved by adding caramel or ivory color to the fondant at the kneading stage until the desired intensity is achieved. Make sure you mix sufficient icing at one time as exact color matches are hard to achieve, and cover the cakes and boards on the same day as the color will fade over time. For these ivory pearls, mix a little topaz luster with dipping alcohol solution to create a thin paste and brush it over the pearls with a paintbrush.

individual cakes

Most of my designs can be transposed onto individual round or square cakes. Other shapes are feasible but trickier to handle. Individual cakes are becoming more fashionable as each guest has his or her own perfectly presented miniature cake, and they are suitable for a variety of occasions. If you are planning a more intimate wedding, include a larger top-tier cake so you can perform the cutting ceremony. (Refer to the guide on page 32 for planning numbers and size of tiers.)

Tip Individual square cakes give you less wastage than round cakes, which are stamped out of a large square cake. If the cakes are to be filled with buttercream, sandwich the large 2 halves together before cutting out the individual cakes.

bumble bees

you will need

25 individual round cakes covered with marzipan and fondant

3-tier stand—10-, 12- and 14-inch hexagonal tiers covered with fondant

yellow, black and white gum paste

½-inch rose cutter for the wings

sugar glue

marking tools

3½ oz. royal icing

black food coloring

pastry bags

no 1.5 tip

10-ft. length of ⅝-inch width green polka-dot ribbon

These are a firm favorite – cute bumble bees with a green-and-white polka-dot ribbon. This cake would be suitable for a child's birthday or christening. Have boxes ready for the guests to take their cake home at the end of the party.

Make the bumble bees' bodies from an elongated ball of yellow paste. Roll the black paste out very thinly and cut narrow black strips and fix these in position over the bumble bees' bodies. Roll out the white gum paste and use a single rose petal cutter to make the wings. Fix these into position with sugar glue. Use a marking tool for the mouth and pipe 2 black eyes. Fix a bumble bee on each individual cake and secure a length of ribbon around each one. Assemble cakes on the stand.

numbers

you will need

25 individual round cakes covered with marzipan and red fondant

3-tier stand—8-, 11- and 14-inch round tiers covered with red fondant

16½-ft. length of ⅝-inch width colored ribbon

3½ oz. royal icing

black food coloring

pastry bags

no. 3 tip

Colored fondant, which I have also used to cover the stand, works well on these individual cakes. The board has been edged in the same ribbon as I have used around the cakes. This cake is a nice idea for a milestone birthday.

Surround each iced cake with a length of ribbon, securing it in position at the back with royal icing. Hand pipe a number on the top of each cake with black royal icing using a pastry bag fitted with a no. 3 tip. Attach ribbon around each tier of the stand and arrange individual iced cakes around it.

summer garden

you will need

25 individual round cakes covered with
marzipan and white fondant

6-inch round cake covered with marzipan
and white fondant

4-tier hexagonal stand—8-, 10-, 12- and
14-inch tiers covered with white fondant

16½-ft. length of ⅝-inch width white ribbon

6½-ft. length of ¼-inch width lilac ribbon

7 oz. royal icing

pastry bags and no. 1.5, 2 and 3 tips

paintbrushes

wooden picks

sponge, cut into small pieces

ball tool and foam pad

waxed paper

⅓ oz. cocoa butter

food color dust

3½ oz. gum paste

lilac and green food colors

1¼-inch rose cutter

1¼-inch calyx cutter

sugar glue

fresh flowers to dress

These individual cakes feature various
decorations and techniques covered in this book
– ribbon loops, sugar rose buds, hand-painted
flowers and royal-iced butterflies – and I have
added a larger full tiffany pearl cake (see page
45) on the top. This is a lovely idea for a more
intimate wedding as the bride and groom have a
cake for the cutting ceremony.

Decorate 5 mini cakes with white and lilac ribbon
loops (see page 49), 5 with sugar butterflies (see
page 125), 5 with hand-painted pansies (using the
template on page 150 and instructions on page 56),
5 with white rose buds and 5 with lilac rose buds
(see page 87). Surround each cake with a length of
the wider ribbon overlaid with narrow ribbon, fixing
at the back with royal icing. For the top tier, pipe a
full tiffany pearl design on the cake as shown using
a no. 2 tip and white royal icing. Arrange the
individual cakes on the lower 3 tiers of the stand
and the full tiffany pearl cake on the top tier. Dress
the top of the cake with flowers.

> **Tip** I have specified a no. 4 tip as the
> aperture is sufficiently large for a small
> paintbrush to be inserted to release the polka
> dot. The gum paste dries and sets very
> quickly so fix the polka dots onto the cakes as
> you make them.

polka dots

you will need

25 individual square cakes covered with
marzipan and white fondant

3-tier stand—8-, 11- and 14-inch round
tiers covered with white fondant

10-ft. length of ⅝-inch width blue ribbon

royal icing

rolling pin

2 oz. dusky pink gum paste

2 oz. powder blue gum paste

2 oz. aqua green gum paste

no. 4 tip

thin paintbrush

sugar glue

Decorate your individual cakes with
large colorful polka dots for a fun
design. Change the colors to
complement your theme or use
different shapes, such as stars for a
Christmas theme or confetti shapes
for a wedding.

Surround each iced cake with a
length of ribbon secured in position
with royal icing. Roll out the gum
paste and use the bottom of a no. 4
plain tip to cut out polka dots. Push
the end of a small paintbrush
through the tip to release the polka
dot and fix into position on the cake
with sugar glue. Arrange the
individual cakes on the stand.

cake templates

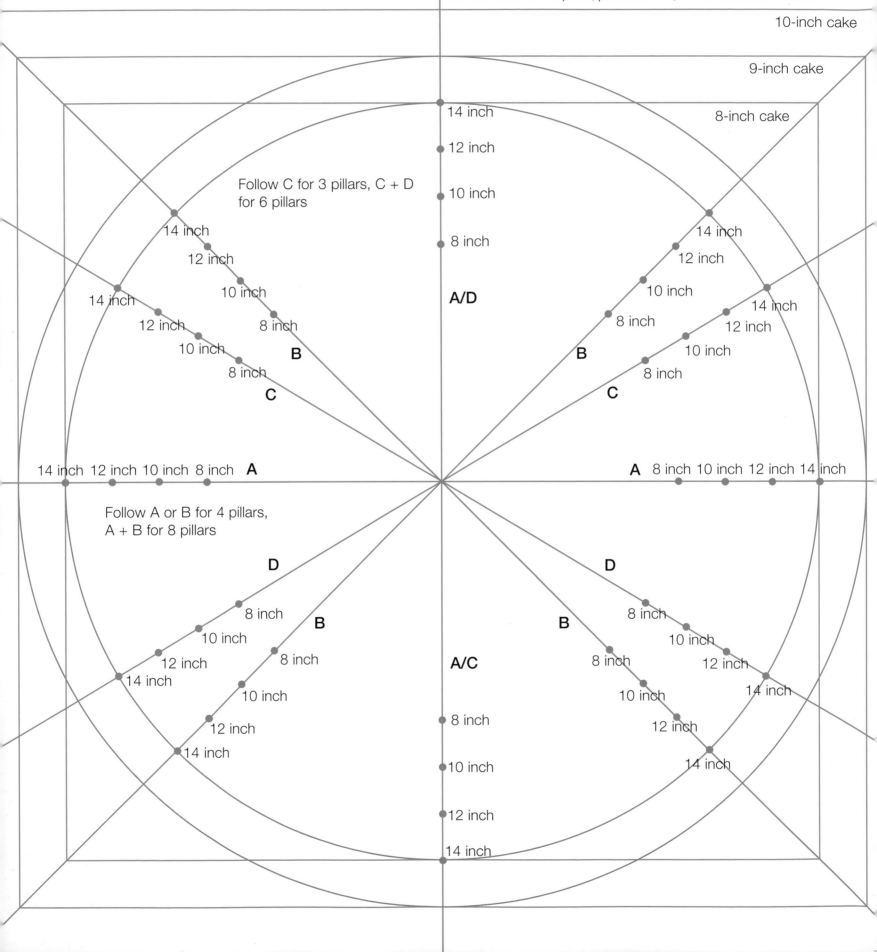

MARKING PILLARS ON A CAKE

see pages 36–7

For round and square cakes up to 10 inches use 4 pillars, positioned at A or B. For larger cakes use 8 pillars, positioned at A and B. For hexagonal and heart-shaped tiers use either 3 or 6 pillars, positioned at C, D or a combination of both.

10-inch cake

9-inch cake

8-inch cake

14 inch

12 inch

10 inch

8 inch

Follow C for 3 pillars, C + D for 6 pillars

14 inch

12 inch

10 inch

8 inch

14 inch

12 inch

10 inch

8 inch

A/D

14 inch

12 inch

10 inch

8 inch

14 inch

12 inch

10 inch

8 inch

B

B

C

C

14 inch 12 inch 10 inch 8 inch   A

A   8 inch 10 inch 12 inch 14 inch

Follow A or B for 4 pillars,
A + B for 8 pillars

D

D

8 inch

10 inch

12 inch

14 inch

8 inch

10 inch

12 inch

14 inch

B

B

8 inch

10 inch

8 inch

10 inch

12 inch

14 inch

A/C

8 inch

10 inch

12 inch

14 inch

PAINTED ORCHID

see page 56

BIRDS OF PARADISE

see page 60

BALLERINA FAIRY

see page 59

LACE BRUSH EMBROIDERY

see page 55

INDIVIDUAL CHRISTMAS

see page 102

BIRTHDAY CLOWN

see page 110

INDIVIDUAL PANSY

see page 143

FLOODED BUTTERFLIES

see page 125

FLEUR-DE-LIS

see page 126

I have found the following to be the most accurate way to ensure that the design lines up perfectly on each tier. Measure the circumference of the tier accurately using ribbon and divide this circumference into 6. Adapt the given template so it fits exactly by stretching or condensing the scrolls slightly. Align the base of a long sheet of waxed paper against the base of the template. Using a waterproof black felt-tip pen (pencil will mark the cake), trace the first sixth of the template. Flip the waxed paper over and line up to draw the next sixth. This will provide one symmetrical copy of the design. Repeat until the design has been drawn a total of 6 times to provide 3 full symmetrical copies of the design.

FABERGÉ 4-TIER

see page 130

For a round cake you will need to measure the circumference accurately using ribbon. Divide the ribbon into 4 by folding it in half then in half again. Starting at the back and base of the cake, mark both ends of a quarter length of ribbon, then move it around the cake until all 4 quarters are accurately marked. Position the template centrally between two of the points and scribe. Repeat for the whole tier.

SECOND TIER

THIRD TIER

BASE TIER

TOP TIER

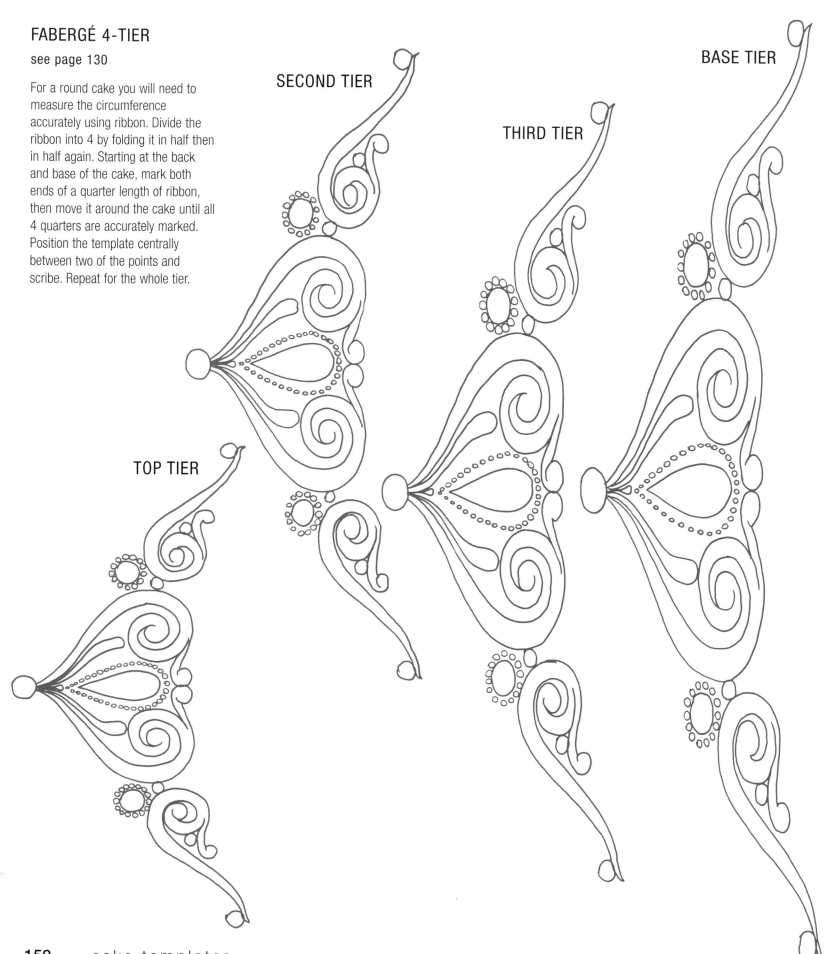

ART DECO
see page 134

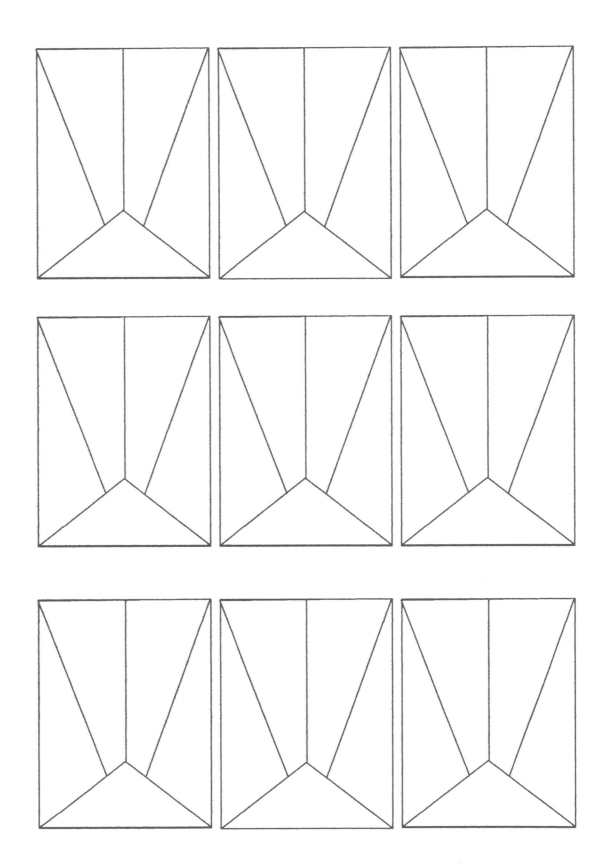

CATLIA LACE

see page 52

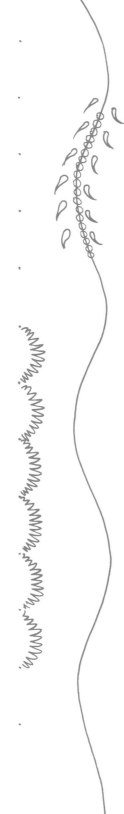

BLACK-PEARL TIARA

see page 138

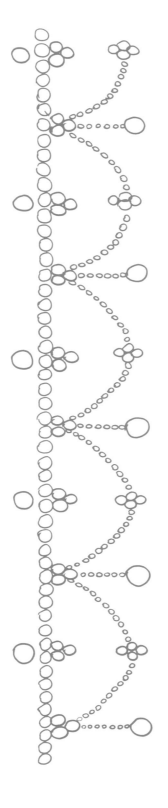

VANITY FAIR

see page 133

ABCDEFGHIJKLM
NOPQRSTUVWXYZ

abcdefghijklmnopqrstuvwxyz

ABCDEFGHIJKLM
NOPQRSTUVWXYZ

1234567890
1234567890

useful addresses

Beryl's Cake Decorating & Pastry
Supplies
P. O. Box 1584
North Springfield, VA 22151
Phone: 1-800-488-2749/
1-703-256-6951
Fax: 1-703-750-3779
www.beryls.com

The Broadway Panhandler
477 Broome Street
New York, NY 10013
Phone: 1-212-966-3434/
1-866-COOKWARE
Fax: 1-212-966-9017
www.broadwaypanhandler.com

Kitchen Krafts
P.O. Box 422-ORD
Waukon, Iowa   52172-0442
Phone: 1-800-776-0575 /
1-563-535-8000
Fax: 1-800-850-3093/
1-563-535-8001
www.kitchenkrafts.com

New York Cake & Baking
56 West 22nd Street
New York, NY 10010
Phone: 1-212-675-2253/
1-800-942-2539
Fax: 1-212-675-7099
www.nycake.com

Pattycakes, Inc.
34-55 Junction Blvd.
Jackson Heights, NY 11372
Phone: 1-718-651-5770/
1-866-999-8400
www.pattycakes.com

Sweet Celebrations Inc.
(Formerly Maid of Scandinavia)
P.O. Box 39426
Edina, MN 55439-0426
Phone: 1-952-943-1508/
1-800-328-6722
www.sweetc.com

The Ultimate Baker
11616 West White Road
Spokane, WA 99224
Phone: 1-866-285-COOK(2665)
Fax: 1-225-410-9048
www.cooksdream.com

Wilton Industries
2240 West 75th Street
Woodridge, IL 60517
Phone: 1-630-963-1818/
1-800-794-5866
Fax: 1-630-963-7196/
1-888-824-9520
www.wilton.com

index

acknowledgments

I have heard it said that 'Everyone has a book in them' and for me that book has always been about cakes! To see a collection of my spectacular cakes published is truly 'the icing on the cake'. It has been made possible with a little help from my friends:

Firstly, I would like to thank my amazing team – past and present – at Little Venice Cake Company: Andrea Markham for flapping your cuffs and assisting with the chocolate cakes; Bee Davies for bringing the character designs to life in sugar; Christine Lee for preparing the sugar flowers; Julie Anne Deane, 'back down under' with Clint and Baba; Amanda Sherlock and Rosie Crichton for keeping me on the straight and narrow.

I am humbled to work with such a talented publishing team: a huge thank you to Jacqui Small for giving me the wonderful opportunity to indulge in my passion and to Kate John for orchestrating this entire project. Thank you Maggie Town for your most expert and discerning eye for design and layout – I love it; thank you Anne McDowall for decrypting and editing my text and learning the names of the cakes; and a special thank you to Janine Hosegood for your outstanding photography. Thank you all for plowing through so many cakes!

I am honored and privileged to work in an industry with so many talented event organizers, party planners, banqueting teams, caterers and florists. The support and belief of so many has helped to propel LVCC to become the prestigious company it is today. I would particularly like to thank Neil Birks, Rob Van Helden and Paul Thomas for your most beautiful flowers and James Partridge for allowing me to adopt Claridge's as my home from home.

A very heartfelt thank you to my family: my parents Ralph and Celia for being there, always, and to Greg and Tanti Max, to whom I dedicate the bumble bees.

Finally, I am hugely grateful to Marie-Louise Sessions (née Wilson), my A-level lecturer, for asking me to decorate her wedding cake when I was 17. Thank you for your belief in me, and the incentive that gave me to discover my career.